BURIED MEMORIES

BURIED MEMORIES

DAVID MARCUS

Marino Books is an imprint of Mercier Press
Douglas Village, Cork
Email: books@mercierpress.ie
Website: www.mercierpress.ie

Trade enquiries to CMD Distribution
55A Spruce Avenue, Stillorgan Industrial Park
Blackrock, County Dublin
Tel: (01) 294 2560; Fax: (01) 294 2564
E-mail: cmd@columba.ie

ISBN 186023 157 8
10 9 8 7 6 5 4 3 2 1

A CIP record for this title is available
from the British Library

Mercier Press receives financial assistance from
the Arts Council/An Chomhairle Ealaíon

Printed in Ireland by ColourBooks, Baldoyle Industrial Estate, Dublin 13

Contents

For my sister, Nella

Prologue

The time to write one's autobiography, if only for oneself, is late in life. However, its drawback is that on the page it reads as if one has written one's own extended obituary. What's more, another drawback follows: time has passed, yet one is still in the world and wondering what to do. To be or not to be, that was my question. What next then, for once the euphoria of writing my first autobiography and seeing it published had faded away, I felt as if whatever was left of my future had been converted into a mere appendage.

Such a conversion had to be reversed. I recalled that when, in 1948, the Israeli government announced the foundation of the State of Israel, what followed was called the War of Independence, a war in which they revealed their secret weapon. It was 'No Alternative'. I decided to adopt that weapon myself and reanimate my future, but despite all my efforts, I failed to awaken in my mind even the glimmer of an idea. The only thing happening was that time kept passing so emptily that I found myself thinking about a second volume of autobiography. Not yet about its material but, keeping myself to first things first, I wondered about a prologue. To cover up the audacity of trying to write a second volume of autobiography, its prologue would have to be as reserved and unobtrusive as the quiet opening of a door.

Early in life I had learned that too much cogitation was an activity my mind rebelled against. The longer I thought, the more

it transmitted to me only tired images of muddle-headed, sloga-
nised strike-banners. At that point I would lie back and pretend
to sleep, knowing it would work away on its own and, like an old
Talmudic debater, would in due course suddenly wake me up with
an enticingly intriguing suggestion. Which it did; and with char-
acteristic craftiness what it now came up with was a line of poetry,
In my beginning is my end, the opening line of 'East Coker', one of
T. S. Eliot's Four Quartets.

I was in my late teens when I first read *Four Quartets,* having
some years earlier come upon, and been enchanted by, 'The Love
Song of J. Alfred Prufrock'. That poem whipped up my Eliot period, until I made two surprisingly disenchanting discoveries in his
poetry. The first was that although his words sang, they didn't
always reveal their meaning. The second was that he appeared to
be an anti-Semite. However, the young Jew I was, who had quickly been captured by literature and music, had soon realised that it
was foolish of me to deprive myself of any great art simply because
its creator was a lesser man. And perhaps it was the very virulence
of the composer, Wagner's, anti-Semitism that convinced me I
must strive not to answer prejudice with prejudice; that, and the
gesture of the world-renowned violinist, Yehudi Menuhin, the first
Jewish musician to give concerts in Germany after the end of the
Second World War. There was, too, the philosopher, Nietzsche,
an amateur pianist and a composer for whom music was life's greatest gift, and who regarded Wagner as his god when, at the age of
twenty-four, he first heard the latter's music. Arranging to meet
him, the two became the closest of friends, so much so that Wagner made him his disciple and a permanent resident in his house
with a room of his own.

Why did this association lodge in my mind? It was because for
quite some time I had been lead to believe that the Nazi ideology
was based on Nietzsche's *Übermensch,* until I learned that the
loathsome ideology was a distortion of the philosopher's concept,
and that his avowed hatred of anti-Semitism was one of the main

reasons he ended his friendship with Wagner.

Eliot's anti-Jewish comments did not immediately make me shy away from accepting *In my beginning is my end* as the opening words of this prologue. What preyed on my mind was a niggle that if I did use it, some crumb of incongruity might well stick in the prologue's craw. The route I had been mapping in my first volume of autobiography was to retread a particular path in my life from its beginning to its fated destination. Obviously I could not repeat any of its milestones, apart perhaps from the previously omitted – because forgotten – odd raconteurable diversions from impromptu byway discussions. Indeed, later in 'East Coker', Eliot himself said, 'There is, it seems to us,/At best, only a limited value/In the knowledge derived from experience'. Agreed, for the limited value of some trifling, though entertaining experiences, is worth no more than the small coin of long-lost recollections, and is not for re-spending. *In my beginning is my end* would have been the perfect harbinger of the prologue to my first volume, but to use it now for a second one would be opening the door into the wrong room, a dusty mausoleum of no longer recountable tales. In some other room, I hoped, there must be an anthology of new memories, real or imagined.

An autobiography, any autobiography, is a record of things and thoughts. The things are one's actualisations, hard facts; the thoughts are the fantasies, whims, ideas, figments, daydreams, pipe-dreams, castles in the air – all the spirits of one's mind games. They constantly wait around until one is tired, or dozy from old age, and then mind takes over matter. Which was just what my own mind kept insisting in my search for the perfect opening line to this prologue. Back it kept coming, the opening line of 'East Coker', *In my beginning is my end*, back as a ghost either to be reborn or to haunt me. I fought with it as Jacob had wrestled with an angel, until the words scrambled in defeat, faded and departed. 'But wait,' I called, awakening with a start, for suddenly I knew its message. In my beginning was my end, that encapsulated the story of my first volume of autobiography, so logically it was from there any second one should take off. In my end is my beginning. Why hadn't I thought of it before? Why should I think of it now? My mind was momentarily clouded with a shadow of suspicion. I took up 'East Coker' again and read it through. When I reached its end, the final line was *In my end is my beginning*. It hadn't been my own thought after all. I had forgotten it with the passage of years, but memory, my old though tired friend, had brought it back, making it mine again.

A Preferred, and Proffered, Prologue

Unfortunately, being encouraged by a new opening line was as near as useless to me, because when thinking about thinking about a further volume of autobiography all I could call up was just one single pathetic recollection, more ancient than merely old. Almost seven decades ago I had decided, indeed determined, to live forever. But very soon, and heartbreakingly, my house of bricks was laid waste when I learned from the Book of Genesis that the Garden of Eden had long been barred and locked, and there was no possible way I could slip in and climb the Tree of Life. The healthy years of childhood, adolescence, coming-of-age, career, marriage and fatherhood kept me happily busy enough with living rather than frittering away time thinking of death. It was there of course, but 'there' was far off in the future. At fifty, one still felt in one's prime and, according to the writer, James Stephens, though women mature at sixteen, men don't make it until they reach sixty.

Stephens was right, but it meant that the arrival of my maturity was an era that gradually, and inexorably, grew into a look-forward-in-anger future. At seventy, I was still reading manuscripts and books, but I felt that the flavour of satisfaction it was giving me was now often nastily soured by an accompanying aftertaste. It didn't take me long to recognise that the aftertaste was in fact the pretaste of non-life. The really foul five-letter word, *death*, was something I couldn't say even to myself. *Gone* was a far more bearable substitute. It didn't fool me of course, but at least it sounded in the inner ear of my mortality a semi-demi-semi note of *ritardando*. Yet how now, and for how long, could I keep myself busy enough to challenge the gnarled old age of Father Time? I needed a new injection, a new drug to re-stimulate the mental excitement I had felt when writing my first volume of autobiography. But I couldn't go to that well again; hadn't I already more or less drained it?

In desperation I turned to the other well I had known – it seemed so long ago – a well inside me not of memories, but of words. In my teens and twenties poetry had flowed, until eventually I accepted that as a poet I would never be more than a maudlin rhymer. By then I had moved on to short stories and, as virtually all short story writers at some stage see themselves as novelists, I too joined the band. Minor successes followed, but that was nearly twenty years ago, at which time I sensibly gave up trying to write another novel. But another novel was the only word-labour worthwhile for me, not with the slightest thought of hoped-for publication, but with the intention of spinning it out and keeping it going for my forever.

Unfortunately, the first question a novel puts to its writer is: 'What am I about?' And I had to face it: what I always seemed to write about were Irish–Jewish characters and their lives. How could I possibly write a novel about anything else when I knew about nothing else? I was an Irish ghetto-Jew, who had had a Jewish Orthodox upbringing, had hardly any Jewish friends in youth (the Cork community then numbered only about four hundred men, women and children) and had never felt able to bond with any Christian acquaintance. If the novel had to be an Irish–Jewish one, could I tackle a task of so much invention and almost endless length if I wanted it to continue throughout the fair span of years I hoped for? I felt it would be beyond me. If I wanted an alternative, then I had to think, yet again, about another volume of autobiography. So Eliot's My *end is my beginning* took stand once more in my mind as the opening door to a second volume of memories, but its infinitesimal chink was black, more pitch than the shadow of a shade and it left me dumb and dememoried.

When one needs a doctor, one goes to a doctor; when one needs a consultant, one consults. I searched out the work of the renowned biographer of Shaw, Michael Holroyd, and found the gem of analysis that flooded my mind with light: 'Though it still has its uses as a reference work, biography is no longer an inventory of facts suspended between a chronology and sources. We know the value of dreams and fantasies, the shadow of a life that isn't lived but lingers within people, and that the lies we tell are part of the truth we live.' So far, so good, but for me the difficulty presented by the analysis was that it dealt with biography. Nevertheless, clearly the prescription could just as helpfully be applied to autobiography.

Almost immediately the dam burst. Within days I came across a second jewel – this of information – from the critic, Harold F. Brooks: 'Proust takes as the starting-point, in his recovery of time past and gone, his moments of involuntary memory.' But I had my doubts. Involuntary memory was a trick of the mind that I might have welcomed if I could for one moment have believed that for the rest of my life it would, day by day, mould for me my own gems of involuntary memory. And then suddenly my own doubts were startlingly dispelled by that Irish–Jewish novel I had thought I might have to tackle instead of my second volume of autobiography.

How often does a novel take off solely because a bare title erupts in a writer's mind, unbidden? It happened to me, just when I needed it: 'The Last Jew in Cork'. Cork was my hometown and by the millennium year the Jewish community comprised only a few dozen people, among whom there were not even ten males over *barmitzvah* age required to make a *quorum* for communal prayer and the reading of the Torah. The time was fast approaching when there wouldn't be a single Jew left in Cork, after more than a century. My novel would have to imagine and create the last one. I saw this last Jew as very old. If he ever had a wife, she would be dead now. And what about possible children? I could work that and much more into a long, slow novel of invention. But why invent only him? Just a single and solitary imagined character might give me little relief and soon both I and he would begin to nod on every page. If the last Jew in Cork was to be alive in my mind, couldn't his life be written side by side with a second volume of autobiography? I could forget Eliot's *In my end is my beginning*. I would have Proust's inspired gift invoking my own involuntary memories. And Proust, too, was a Jew. So it all fitted: another volume of autobiography backpacking the story of Cork's last Jew.

I was wondering what name I would give him, this last Jew in Cork, when his phone rang. It rang for some time before he decided to answer it. He presumed it would be a wrong number. It had to be a wrong number – unless it was one of his dead, old friends phoning him from the grave to tell him to hurry up, they were all missing him.

'Yes,' he said, no enquiring note in his voice. He had forgotten to say 'Hello'. Another thing that had slipped an old man's mind.

'Is that Mr Cohen? Mr Aaron Cohen?' It was a female voice.

'Who are you? What do you want?'

'I hope I haven't disturbed you, Mr Cohen. My name is Catherine O'Driscoll.'

'I don't know you. What do you want?'

'I work for the *Irish Examiner*, Mr Cohen, and my editor is very anxious that I interview you for the paper. We want to publish an interview to celebrate your ninetieth birthday, and to honour the last, only living member of Cork's Jewish community.'

Aaron was flabbergasted. He didn't know what he could possibly say. How should he answer? Should he put the phone down? He had to think.

'Who are you? How do you know my name?'

'Catherine, that's my name, Catherine O'Driscoll. And I found that your name was in the phone book, Mr Cohen. That's how I knew where to reach you.'

Aaron said nothing to that.

The girl said nothing either. She didn't want to pressurise or upset him. An old man, nearly ninety, he mightn't have all his marbles at that age. And she didn't want to spoil her chance. She hadn't been long with the paper and very much wanted to impress the editor.

'It wouldn't be any trouble, Mr Cohen. An interview is very easy. I'd just talk to you. About your life. Your life in Cork, you wouldn't have to come to our office. I'd do the interview in your own home. At your own convenience, Mr Cohen. When would suit you?'

Aaron still didn't reply.

She feared he might say no, so she thought it best to give him some time to consider her suggestion.

'I'll tell you what, Mr Cohen. You think about it and I'll ring you again tomorrow. Same time. Wouldn't that be the best, Mr Cohen?'

Yes, he thought, yes. I don't know what to say.

'Yes, tomorrow, tomorrow.' I needn't answer the phone was what immediately ran through his mind.

'That's great, Mr Cohen. I'll phone you tomorrow. I'd love to meet you. It would be an honour. Thanks again.'

The call ended.

The name 'Aaron Cohen' just came to me without having to think about it. In the Bible, Aaron, his brother, Moses, and their sister, Miriam, were the three most important Israelites, and they led their people out of Egyptian bondage. Aaron became the first of the priests, and his descendants were recognised as the priestly caste, known in Hebrew as *Kohanim*.

After the destruction of the temple, the time came when proof of one's priestly descent was no longer possible, so a Jew who bore the name 'Cohen' could claim to be a *kohen*, a priest. Even today, any Jew who believes himself to be descended from *Kohanim* could claim priestly status.

My first recognition of such a person as a *kohen* in the Cork community came about when, little older than a child, I was regularly brought to synagogue services. On special occasions, a *kohen* would stand with his back to the Ark of the Law while he gave the congregation the priestly blessing. His face would be hidden from them, concealed under his voluminous prayer-shawl, completely enshrouding him from the back of his head to the tips of his outstretched arms and hands. From under the shawl would be heard the prayers as his voice and arms rose and fell to the soulful rhythms of his blessings.

The first time I saw this extraordinary appearance, its motion and shape was like that of a head-nodding alligator, an image that frequently recurs to me in all its eidetic vividness.

If Aaron Cohen ever fulfilled that priestly duty it could never be his again, for there were no other Cork Jews left to be blessed, no longer a synagogue where a service could be conducted, and no lost descendants to locate their ancestors' graves in the overgrown and abandoned Jewish burial ground high up above the river Lee on the Old Blarney Road that heard only the cold, wild winds and the skirling, uncanorous rain.

The Blood of Memory

Memo – the word, that is – is the offspring of its old man, memory, and it is there to satisfy the old man. The fact is, however, that this old man is not only its own boss, but yours and mine too. And what now and again it likes to indulge is to play the fool – we being the real fools. Forgetting becomes more and more common to us mortals, especially when we get older. Most people sooner or later complain about such an affliction, and eventually those of us burdened with the necessity of always having to remember vital information – names, addresses, telephone numbers, directions, messages etc – have to wed ourselves to a pocket-notebook in which all those business and social lifelines are recorded. But what if one has forgotten to remember even that there is something important to remind oneself of? The only answer is to adopt the certain daily morning routine of reading every item in the pocket-book not already crossed out.

I never carried nor possessed such a pocket-book – I resented making myself a slave of a mechanistic morning routine. I do, however, keep a small notebook in which I write the meanings of words I didn't previously know; not that that's of much help, because learning them off doesn't make them stay in the memory.

Ah, memory, the word itself reminds me of something I now can never forget.

Early in 2001 I was having morning coffee with a promising new writer who had earlier shown me her first short stories. I liked them and asked to see more, and at this meeting she gave me her latest story. I glanced at its beginning. The first sentence puzzled me. I read it again, but still couldn't comprehend it. Each word was perfectly familiar and I knew what each meant, but reading the words in succession conveyed nothing to me. I shook my head, and in bewilderment looked at the writer.

'Is there something wrong?' she asked.

'Not with what you've written. But I can't make sense of it. Somehow it's my own fault. I can't make sense of myself.'

'Are you ill? Do you feel ill?'

'I feel … funny … not ill, just … peculiar. Sort of … queer. As if somehow reality isn't real.'

'I think you *are* ill. I think you'd better go home.' I couldn't reply. I just nodded my head, got up and went home. Fortunately my wife was in. She told me that a lady had phoned to let her know that I had felt peculiar and she was worried about it.

I tried to tell my wife what had happened, but my account was composed of silences rather than words. I couldn't make sense to her. She phoned our doctor but he was booked up and couldn't call until after six. When he came, he asked me to tell him how I felt, but it was still difficult for me to explain. He examined me, and then advised my wife to take me to hospital. We got there at eight o'clock and sat in Casualty until four a.m., when I was registered, examined by a doctor and given a bed.

Next morning I was informed that they would take a scan of my head. The scan was taken, I went back to bed, and after a while a consultant came to me. He asked me some questions which I tried to answer, but I couldn't properly verbalise what I wanted to say. He explained that a blood vessel in my head had sustained a very slight, momentary burst, and the blood had come into contact with the left side of my brain, the memory side. As a result, I would have some trouble in communicating exactly what I wanted to say because I wouldn't be able to remember the necessary words. This, evidently, was something that many older people suffer, and full recovery could be expected, though it would very probably take anything from six to twelve months to gradually get back to normality. I was kept in hospital for a week, two more scans were taken and the consultant saw me again before I was allowed home. He instructed me not to try to read or write for the next six weeks or so and then to take things very slowly when starting work again.

At home all I could do was look at television, listen to music and practise the piano. Reading music presented no difficulty, its notes being a language of signs, not words. At such a time, it was dearer even than speech to me, just as it always was to the writer, Vikram Seth, as he declared in the author's note to his novel, *An Equal Music*. In the first few weeks, however, I was more and more bored, and very much more angry. I felt quite well, but I could do next to nothing. The total break in my usual routine filled me with a new-life emptiness. I called it that so as to avoid thinking of the emptiness as a permanent non-life one. I feared that otherwise the closed door, behind which my memory loitered, might open momentarily only to show me that on the other side was still nothing but darkness. So, after about three weeks I took up the newspaper and tried to read it. Useless. I could understand each separate word just as when the affliction first struck, but they still failed to link with each other or with me. Another few weeks and my patience snapped. With a sudden but silent snap of a Proustian involuntary memory I recalled the statement by the writer, Milan Kundera, that 'For memory to function well, it needs constant practice'. I didn't delay a moment. I took up a book, opened it, and started to read. At last it began to make sense, admittedly with a little difficulty, but day by day everything became easier.

So how long did it take for my memory to resume its normal function and effectiveness? The fact is that it never did. Nowadays every day, often more than once, a word I particularly want to use to express an idea in my mind will elude me for a lengthy period, sometimes until later in the day, sometimes until even the next day. Perhaps I had pushed my memory too soon, too hard. Perhaps old age, too, had its finger in the pie, allowing it to work only part-time. Why is it that although twenty-five or more years have passed since I first found myself meeting a Stygian gap when trying to greet a friend or relation by name – other people I spoke to about it revealed that it was a well-known affliction for them too – but why now should both uncommon and commonplace words have started to adopt habits of absent-on-leave appellations?

Psychiatrists would say that I forget the names of people I don't like, or am afraid of, or have a grudge against, or don't want to know, or some such cockeyed theory. But that's too easy an explanation, too obvious. Doctors might say that there's some malfunction in my memory processes. Why does it affect only the names of people I know and not the names of people I don't know personally, such as film stars, sports stars, prominent politicians, public figures, etc? Show me a photograph of anyone of any eminence whom I should recognise, and I'll stick the right moniker on him or her immediately. And why, too, are only names blotted out? Why not numbers, dates, facts, messages, appointments?

Whatever the reason, my failing is a constant embarrassment. I can somehow disguise it in a one-to-one encounter, but well-attended gatherings are constant ordeals. And how much help is it at a rare function when the standard practice is for everyone to wear a name-badge? Even then it's certain I'm going to be talking to someone I know very well but whose name I just can't recall, and I get nearly cross-eyed trying to steal a glance at his or her badge without making it obvious. As a result I have long ago been forced to become an almost total recluse.

There's only one solution for it: I shall have to wear a badge at all such events with the excuse on it 'I forget names'. If so many people share the same affliction, then why don't we all get together, set up a club and always carry that badge? The one time I suggested it to a good friend who had the same trouble, he laughed and wouldn't take me seriously. Now what in the world is his name?

Anyway, in the meantime I have someone else on my mind to worry about and I have no trouble with *his* name, Aaron Cohen, the ninety-year-old last Jew in Cork. What sort of memories do I propose to extract from him is what he is already asking me. Of course I have to ask them of myself first, but even before I could get down to that problem, my mad memory suddenly barged in and to my astonishment revived recollections of two events that had been completely lost in my mind for over half a century.

The first goes back to London in 1946. My visit was connected with the impending publication of the first issue of the *Irish Writing* quarterly, but I also had in mind the idea of approaching three renowned British-based writers to ask if they would each write a new short story for an annual story magazine. The first one on my list was the then extremely popular and highly regarded novelist, Louis Golding, who was also a poet and a writer who, in 1933, had written a study of James Joyce.

He was born in 1895, in Manchester, and what drew me to him was his novel, *Magnolia Street*, published in 1931, a story of a typical street in a provincial city whose inhabitants were Jews on one side, Gentiles on the other. It's hardly surprising that I don't now remember one character from it, but it's pleasant to imagine it as a distant antecedent of my recreation of Cork's 'Jewtown' in my novel, *A Land Not Theirs*, written over fifty years later.

I have absolutely no memory of how I contacted Louis Golding who was living in London, but he must have agreed that I could call on him. His residence was a large, elegant semi-mansion in a quiet, broad and leafy suburban road – which is how I see it now in my mind's eye. He answered the door himself and accompanied me to his upstairs study, one wall of the stairway being almost overpoweringly festooned with paintings. The study was equally impressive, and its dimensions, when I think of my approximately six by four feet editorial office in my Cork home, must have made me feel like an interloper rather than a real editor. I imagine I would have told him how much I had liked his *Magnolia Street* and how it had made me approach him for a short story. Before giving me an answer, I remember we had some sort of general conversation – I have no doubt he'd have guessed from my name that I was Jewish – and then he dealt with my request. In the kindest possible way he made it plain that my idea was really a non-starter, and that if I were to write to his agent, the fee requested would certainly shock me. I realised that – to put it bluntly – I was making a fool of myself, but at least Louis Golding had let me down gently.

The other event, which took place in May–June 1947 would have remained dead and buried had I not recently found a copy – the only issue ever to appear – of *Shandon: Cork's Own Magazine No. 1*. It was published from the same address as that of the *Irish Writing* quarterly. Its aim – so said its introduction – was 'to reflect Cork life, to entertain, and to appear regularly'. It had twenty-eight pages, including a woman's page, a crossword puzzle with a £5 prize for the first correct answer, some general local articles including 'The Story of Father Prout' by David O'Meara (who must surely have been me), a ghost story by David Maher (me again), and the sporting career up to then of Jack Lynch by 'Onlooker' – no, definitely not me. The price of *Shandon* was sixpence!!

Glory days, of a sort.

The Milk of Human Kindness

No further involuntary memories erupted, either because if any more existed, they were coming along only at their own meanderthal pace, or more likely because at that point Aaron began to re-occupy my mind.

To a writer, someone who exists only in his mind can quickly become a friend, and frequently, created characters develop much of their own independence. Aaron had that in spades, and wasted little time in letting me know how he had decided to handle Miss O' or Mrs O' when she'd phone him the next morning.

After her first call, he had spent the rest of the day quarrelling with himself about the whole idea of being interviewed for a newspaper just because his ninetieth birthday was approaching. Plenty other people would soon be celebrating their ninetieth birthday but would they be written about in the paper? Of course not. Yet I am to be honoured – he emphasised it, with sharp, biting sarcasm, *honoured* – just because I'm a Jew, the last one in Cork. What am I? The last of the Mohicans? It was all so preposterous. Suppose he let her interview him and he died the next day. It could happen, couldn't it?

That's what he had asked his doctor not long ago.

'Mr Cohen,' the doctor said. 'I could die myself tomorrow. Anyone can, and some people will. But I don't expect you or me to pop off like that.'

'Look, we both know my health isn't one hundred per cent.

And I'm on the brink of ninety. More like on the edge, isn't it? Whereas you're only about sixty.'

'Mr Cohen, if I could make you sixty, I would, but I can't produce a miracle.'

'Who's asking for a miracle? I don't want to be younger, I want to be older.'

The doctor laughed. 'You never lost it, Mr Cohen. It's great to keep your sense of humour.'

Aaron snorted. 'That's not *my* joke. I read it a few years ago, in a book some Jewish writer wrote.'

'I might have guessed it, Mr Cohen. Typical Jewish humour, always wry, especially when against themselves.'

Come the end of that evening Aaron was still grumbling away, still unable to decide whether he'd agree to that female's interview. For him the end of every evening was always the worst time of the day. Alone in an empty house, only an empty bed waiting, only night-noises to be heard, only little sleep to kill the hours, another day to face with only a past to live with – what was it all for, what was it all about? And that phone call to expect – that female, woman, lady, girl, whatever she was – the one from the paper. He heard her voice. Was he imagining it, or mixing it up with his wife's? He thought of her every day, every night, how could he not? But how hard it was, to hear and to bear. Forget it for tonight. Try to sleep. Think of tomorrow's phone call. Tell her they could meet. Let her think he'd agree to an interview. Maybe he would, maybe he wouldn't. O'Something or other. Miss O' or Mrs O'? That's how he'd address her. That way he'd find out whether she was single or married. To ask her straight out would be too personal, too indiscreet. He believed in old-fashioned manners. His wife had admired it. But nowadays no one cared about manners, especially the young. He hoped his visitor would be a married woman, he felt he'd find it easier to talk to her than to a young, single girl. Not that he'd decide there and then to let her interview him. Supposing he did let her, and he died the next day, they wouldn't want to waste the interview, would they? They'd probably just use it as an obituary. And he wouldn't be alive to read it. What a *schlimazel* that would be.

Aaron fell asleep smiling. If he could have been awake to feel himself smiling, who knows if it would have made him happy. He used always fall asleep with a smile when his wife turned around to tuck herself into his back.

It was April, and cold, the Jewish month of *Nisan*, when Passover is celebrated. Aaron wouldn't be celebrating it, except in his mind for he'd have no company, and no *matzah*, the unleavened bread. For as long as I lived in my home in Cork, Passover was the festival I most revelled in. The whole story is told in the *Haggadah* – 'The Telling' – and my parents, my brothers and sister and I recited and sang it together at our *Seder* on each of the first two evenings. Its rituals seemed unending, with not unlike a Mardi Gras atmosphere for eight days. Why eight days? Because that was the length of time the Israelites wandered through the wilderness to reach the Red Sea, opened by God for them to traverse and confirm their freedom from slavery under the Pharaohs.

Do any pious Jews nowadays perform during Passover the symbolic re-enactment of the crossing of the sea by pouring water over the floorboards of their home and walking through it? My father never tried that – no doubt my mother would hardly have enjoyed it – but the ritual he always fulfilled was the first one of the festival, and for me the most fascinating of them all. On the morning of Passover eve he would visit every room in the house and leave a crust of bread in a corner. Then at night I would accompany him when he would re-visit every room to collect all the crusts into a package, and next morning he would burn the package in the fire, reciting the necessary blessing. Bread, being leavened, was never allowed in the home at Passover. Because the Israelites had, perforce, to flee Egypt at a moment's notice, they had not the time to bake their bread and so had to carry unleavened bread. Hence *matzah*, the perennial symbol of Passover, sufficient quantities of which were prepared by *kosher* bakers in Britain and the US and exported to Ireland. Indeed, apart from fruit, meat and fish that could be eaten, every food and drink for the long festival had to be specially prepared by *kosher* suppliers under strict rabbinical rules and authorisation. Milk was the one item that presented a problem for us and Cork's Jews during the time when milk was delivered by one's local farmer. He would arrive up in horse and trap every morning, knock on your door with his early morning tattoo and pour from his can into your proffered one as many pints as you needed. Understandably, his cans could not be used for our Passover milk, in all Jewish households every pot, pan, saucepan and can would have been pre-heated, washed, scoured and cleaned for use during the festival. So every year my father, sometimes accompanied by me, would take a few of our made-*kosher* cans to a farm not far out the Lee Road, and we would stand beside the farmer to see a cow being milked straight into our cans.

There came a year when my father decided it was about time I went to the farm by myself. 'When you get married, some day, you'll have your own home and you'll be the one to get the Passover milk.'

I didn't mind. I was pleased to have his trust. And at most, three journeys would be enough to get sufficient milk for the whole Passover week.

'Oh, by the way,' he said, 'we have a new farmer now. He bought the farm from our last fellow and I imagine he knows nothing about Passover. So when he calls tomorrow morning, you'd better have a word with him and tell him the procedure. I'm sure he won't mind. A customer is a customer.'

'What's his name?' I asked.

'Corcoran. Mr Corcoran.' Corcoran, however, turned out to be somewhat younger than our previous farmer. The latter had been an earthy, philosophical bloke, and not without some information on the meaning of Passover. He knew that *kosher* milk meant 'Jews' milk' for Easter, and he had been heard to comment that if all his customers did likewise, it would save him a fair bit on overheads and transport. But Corcoran, how would *he* respond to my request?

Next morning, when he was filling my jug with milk so fresh that it still steamed warm in the chilly April air, I broached the question.

'Mr Corcoran,' I said casually, as if asking him about the weather, 'have you heard of Passover?'

He looked up suddenly and cast a quick glance round, as if he thought it *was* the weather I had asked about.

'Did I hear *what* pass over, Mr Marcus?' he asked curiously.

'No, Mr Corcoran,' I answered quickly, anxious not to get the poor fellow confused before he even met with the real problem. 'Nothing passed over. I asked if you ever heard of Passover? You know, the Jews' Easter.'

'Oh, the Jews' Easter,' he echoed in a broad tone as of recognition. But his eyes were looking at me a trifle doubtfully, and it was obvious he had no notion of what I was talking about.

'Yes, the Jews' Easter, Passover,' I repeated. 'You never heard of it then?'

'I don't know did I hear of it years back,' he essayed guardedly. He was not anxious to admit his ignorance before discovering whether lack of the knowledge was his own fault or not. But his Irish caution was not unlike certain Jewish caution, so I was at home to it on both grounds.

Briefly and carefully I explained to him what Passover was and why I wished to exercise personal supervision over the milk I needed for the festival. He listened, his head down, his eyes examining the bottom of his pint-measure.

'You mean,' he said when I had finished, 'you want to come and milk the cow yourself, Mr Marcus?' There was a note of awe in his voice.

'No, no, certainly not. I'll just bring my can along and watch you milk the cow straight into the can. Would you have any objection to that?' I tried to disguise the doubtful hope in my question.

'And why should I object, Mr Marcus?' rejoined Corcoran enthusiastically.

I knew immediately that his enquiry was purely rhetorical and I could see by the returned light in his eyes that, however unusual my request may have sounded, he was determined to take it in his stride. 'I'll put aside Eileen for you. She's the best milker I have.'

'Oh, I don't mind who does the milking,' I said, magnanimously. Mr Corcoran broke into peals of laughter. 'Wisha, God bless you, Mr Marcus, Eileen is the cow! Eileen Aroon, my prize milch-cow. As to the milking, I'll attend to that meself.'

'There's no need for you to trouble yourself,' I protested.

'No trouble at all, I'd be glad of the chance. I got in those electric things lately, the automatic milking-machines, and since I did I've got a bit out of practice in the old way. So I won't mind getting down to it again.'

'Well, if you insist, Mr Corcoran, that's very good of you,' I said.

There and then we made the necessary arrangements and I bade him goodbye.

My first expedition was on the afternoon of the eve of Passover and Corcoran was all ready for me. He waved, and came towards me across the small farmyard, scattering chickens from his path.

'Ready for you, Mr Marcus,' he smiled, guiding me to a long shed from which a great deal of mooing issued forth. 'It'll only take five minutes.'

At the door of the shed he donned a long, white coat and washed his hands. Then he stretched out each leg – he was wearing heavy gum-boots – and allowed the stream of water to wash the dirt off. All this cleanliness was very impressive and I felt like a visitor about to be brought by a doctor into a fever-stricken hospital ward.

The shed was long and low but there was plenty of light in it, all one side having windows. The cows – maybe thirty or so – faced the other wall, each in her own stall. At their heads were little racks of grass and other greenery, and behind each tail-swishing rump was a steel bar to make sure the occupant could not back out of her stall. Corcoran walked about halfway down the line and I followed him, my ears full of the gentle mooing noises and my nostrils full of the heavy animal odour.

'Here we are now,' Corcoran said, unlatching the bar behind one cow and taking the can from my hand. 'Right now, old girl.'

The cow half-turned her head and rolled an eye at him as he pulled a stool from the wall and patted her side.

'Is that your prize one?' I asked.

'That's right. Good old Eileen Aroon. She's the best milker of the lot.' He put the can underneath her and started to work. For a few moments I watched the jetting white streams ping against the sides of the can and then, as I looked up, my eye was caught by the electrical machinery running along the ceiling.

'Is that the electric-milker above us?' I asked.

'That's it,' he answered without looking up.

'Do you like it?'

'It's good all right. Does a lot of work. I haven't got it long.' Corcoran was not fully won over yet, I thought.

'Do the cows like it?'

'Ah, that's the right question,' he answered, casting a glance at me. 'They didn't at first but I think they're getting used to it now.' He paused, and added with a laugh, 'Like their owner.'

'How did it affect them when you started?'

'They were bad-tempered, and their milk was poor and slow. But it's back to normal again.'

By this time the can was half full and the steam was rising from it.

'But won't this change back to the old style upset Eileen Aroon?' I queried.

'Not her. She don't mind. And anyway, I hand-milked her this morning just to get her used to it again. I won't use the machine on her any more till your Easter is over. Here now, I think this is as much as you'll be able to manage,' as he lifted the can away.

I pushed the cover on, feeling the warm glow of the metal, and walked back along the shed to the door. The cows had quietened down as I turned to thank Corcoran. He was still standing by Eileen Aroon's stall, his head crooked away as if he was lost in thought. Seeing me turn, he hastened to catch up with me.

'Very grateful to you, Mr Corcoran,' I thanked him.

'Sure, 'tis no trouble at all, Mr Marcus,' he said. 'No trouble at all.' But he seemed preoccupied. I went home, satisfied that much had been successfully accomplished.

My second visit, three days later, followed the same pattern, except that again I thought Corcoran had something on his mind. I noticed that when he commenced to milk Eileen Aroon he stopped a moment to examine the liquid in the can. Then he straightened up and gave the cow a playful slap on the belly.

'Wouldn't doubt you, my treasure! I knew you'd not let me down.'

'Was there something wrong?' I asked.

'It was just that some of the others are a bit off colour. A lot of the milk isn't their best. But nothing worries this one. You'll not get better than her in the four provinces of Ireland.'

'What's gone wrong with the others then?' I asked.

'Divil I know,' Corcoran replied. 'It wasn't very much – and it'll pass, no doubt.'

He continued to milk Eileen Aroon, but soon he stopped again and lifted his head.

'What is it?' I asked quickly, fearful that some new mishap would put a stop to our milk for Passover.

'Quare, blashted quare,' was all he answered.

'Is the milk not right, after all?'

'Wisha, the milk is fine. But don't you hear?'

'Hear what? I hear nothing.' I couldn't understand what he meant. Corcoran was right. I hadn't noticed that the other cows had all suddenly grown still. Not a moo was to be heard.

'What's come over them?' I asked.

'Damned if I know,' Corcoran replied, returning to his task. 'But it can't be much if they're not shouting about it.'

If he was satisfied, I certainly was too, and I gave the unusual occurrence no further thought. But when I arrived a few days later for my final visit, Corcoran was far from his easy-going, pleasant self. His face was long and there was a dark stare in his eyes.

'I hope your milk will be good today, Mr Marcus,' he said without preliminary greeting.

'Oh? Something wrong?'

'Well, not with Eileen Aroon – yet. But all the others are giving bad stuff and I fear she might go sour on me too. I don't know what's the matter with them.'

'They seem to have found their voices again anyway,' I commented, nodding towards the shed where there was a great deal of mooing and commotion.

'Wait and see,' Corcoran rejoined enigmatically as he led the way.

I soon found out what he meant by that. Immediately we set foot in the shed, all noise ceased. Not a sound came from the cows. It was uncanny – unnatural.

'What in the world is wrong with them?' I asked in amazement.

'Blowed if I know! Every time I come in, they shut up.'

He walked ahead of me slowly.

'And that's not all,' he said. 'There's something mighty quare going on here.'

We reached Eileen Aroon's stall, and Corcoran gave her rump a thwack. It rang out like a rifle crack in the stillness. Eileen Aroon mooed pleasantly in reply.

'Well, she still seems in fine fettle,' I ventured.

'She does, thanks be for that. Her milk's still good too. Up to this morning, anyway.'

'Whatever is wrong with the others hasn't affected her,' I commented in relief.

Corcoran didn't reply but only looked strangely at me.

'I dunno,' he said slowly and with much reservation.

'Well, her milk is still OK, isn't it?' I asked, looking into the can.

'It's not her milk I'm thinking of,' he answered, half-reluctantly.

'What is it then?' I coaxed.

'Well,' he blurted, 'you can laugh if you like – but every time I turn them out in the field to pasture, they all keep away from Eileen Aroon. If she tries to go with them, they huddle together like a pack of old women and move off from her! I've never seen anything like it.'

I *did* laugh – I had to.

'It may sound funny, Mr Marcus, but there must be some meaning to it.'

'What do you think yourself?' I asked, puzzling over the phenomenon.

Corcoran rubbed his lower lip. 'I've been all my life with animals,' said he. 'I know dogs have intelligence, and horses, but not cows. At least, not till now.'

'What has intelligence got to do with it?'

Corcoran raised his head and jabbed a thumb towards the electric-milkers above us.

'See these things?' he said. 'I told you that at first they didn't like them – not that I'd blame them for that. But now they see me hand-milking Eileen Aroon every day – well – damned if I don't think they're jealous of her and sort of going on strike!'

'Is that what you think?' I asked.

'Well, look what's happened. And listen to them. Quiet as

tombstones just because I've come to milk her. It's – it's too –'

'Human?' I echoed, a strange idea running through my mind. 'What do *you* call it then, Mr Marcus?'

I didn't mean to say what had occurred to me, but I must have been thinking out loud.

'Anti-Semitism,' I muttered.

'Anti-semenism,' Corcoran said, misunderstanding me. 'Is that something to do with artificial insemination, Mr Marcus?'

'No, no,' I hastened to reassure him, 'nothing at all. Perhaps you're right – maybe it's only natural animal jealousy.'

I could hardly explain to him the vague idea that had thrust itself upon me. Besides, it seemed so outlandish, so fantastic.

'Well, I hope they get it over quickly,' Corcoran said as he finished the milking.

As it happens, the cows did get it over quickly. When Corcoran resumed his deliveries to me after Passover, he told me that as soon as he returned to milking Eileen Aroon by electricity the next day, the cows became normal, giving good milk, mooing at him pleasantly, and not shunning Eileen Aroon during pasture time.

'It was nothing serious, Mr Marcus,' he said.

'No,' I agreed, 'nothing serious.'

Nothing serious? Many times since then the case of the persecuted cow has niggled at my mind and I have wondered. Was it what Corcoran suggested – an understandable animal desire for the human touch they had been used to? Perhaps. But, on the other hand, there was that ridiculous suspicion in my mind – could the cows' jealousy of Eileen Aroon have been due to the fact that she was the Chosen Cow? After all, how much do we really know about animal intelligence? Can't cows have prejudices too?

The bizarre occurrence at Corcoran's farm over the Passover milk stayed with me. The experience struck me as ideal for a short story, and some time later I wrote it and called it 'The Case of the

Persecuted Cow'. I knew of an American–Jewish magazine, *The Menorah Journal*, and on 10 October 1956, I submitted the story to them. It was accepted on 26 December of that year, but apart from the acceptance letter, not another word of any sort passed between me and the *Journal*, nor did I even know if my story had appeared in print. Very soon afterwards I emigrated to London and the story dropped completely from my mind.

One day towards the end of 1999 I received a letter from a gentleman in New York whom I didn't know, nor indeed do I remember how he ascertained my Dublin address. He told me that he was leafing through a voluminous collection of letters, documents and manuscripts that had been left by his father, who during his life had been the editor of *The Menorah Journal*. Among the papers was 'The Case of the Persecuted Cow', evidently already set in proof, but for no known reason had never been used. The gentleman asked my permission to show the story to the editor of *Midstream: A Monthly Jewish Review*, whom he knew. Needless to say, I was more than happy to say yes. The story appeared in *Midstream's* issue of May–June 2000.

And the cow jumped over the moon.

A Long-Playing Record

I f you don't want to learn about a past that you had forgotten ever existed, don't mess about in choked up old cupboards. Fortunately, my rummaging revealed nothing that wasn't perfectly innocent, though it did show many signs of naiveté, chance-your-arm foolishness, and manducating mice. What the latter had nibbled at was a 27-page record of my manuscript submissions to papers and magazines from 1945 to 1958 inclusive. The fact that in 1945 I turned twenty-one suggests to me that pages covering my teen years must once have existed too, because I know that even before I left school the writing and publication bugs had already bitten me. And there was also a third biter, for I never forgot there had been a jotter that recorded for a year or so the book titles of my 'serious reading' bug after I gave up, first comics, and then *The Champion* and *Triumph* weeklies. That jotter has never turned up, but how I know it definitely existed is that I still remember the very first book I named in it. It was Ernie O'Malley's *On Another Man's Wound*, published in 1936, and a few years must surely have passed before I obtained it, presumably from Cork Public Library. John McGahern, in an essay in the *Irish Times* on the publication in 2002 of the revised edition of the book, quoted an extract from a letter written by the American poet, Hart Crane, to Malcolm Cowley, from Mexico on 2 June 1921:

I have my most pleasant literary moments with an Irish revolu-
tionary, red-haired friend of Liam O'Flaherty, shot (and not
missed) seventeen times in one conflict and another; the most
quietly sincere and appreciative person, in many ways, whom
I've ever met. It's a big regret that he's Dublin bound again after
three years from home, in a few weeks, Ernie O'Malley by name.
And we drink a lot together, look at frescoes – and agree!

The detailed record of my manuscript submissions told me much
about the myself of that bygone world. I learned about my early
obsession with writing and achieving publication, which latter
determined me to bombard editors with plagues of poems and
stories, a bombardment that reminds me of the ten Old Testament plagues that punished the Pharaohs for persecuting the cap-
tive Jews until they released them. The great majority of my submissions elicited only rejection slips with no word of criticism or
encouragement – sometimes not even the return of my manuscripts despite my provision of a self-addressed, stamped envelope. I had a rule to submit work to at least one publication
every week, and although I sometimes missed out, much more
often than not I greatly exceeded fifty-two submissions per year.
In six of the fourteen years, each of them boasted over one hundred submissions – the figure for 1955 being the record of two hundred and seven. The total submissions for all those years topped
one thousand: over two hundred in Ireland, almost six hundred in
Britain, two hundred in the US, and fifteen in foreign fields.

I doubt that I ever saw many of the British, US, and foreign
magazines with which I chanced my arm. I chased up their addresses and the details of their requirements in various literary
directories, but what I often fell for were their strange names,
such as *Washington Filibuster*, *Adam*, *The Decachord*, *Humor-Esq*,
The Mint, *Furioso*, *The Golden Goose*, *Meanjin*, *Prairie Schooner*,
Halapid and *Botteghe Oscure*.

So what was my tally in the acceptance column over all the

years? Stories were accepted thirty-nine times and poetry on sixty occasions. These figures also include one rather unusual entry. It arose from my submission to *The New Statesman* of a short story which they accepted, and the editor's letter mentioned that it might take some time before they would have sufficient space for it. As *The New Statesman* had always been a favourite of mine – I used to buy it every week – any delay in being included in its contributors did not greatly worry me. Unfortunately however, before the story could be published, the editor – whose name I have forgotten (not Kingsley Martin) – resigned, after which my manuscript was peremptorily returned. Nothing like this had ever happened to me before or since, so I wrote to the new editor – whose name I have gladly forgotten too – telling him that I was sending my story back to him, and that if he consulted his predecessor's files he would find that the story had already been accepted. He didn't reply, just merely sent my manuscript back on its second return journey with a cheque attached to it. That story later went to other publications but perhaps it now had a jinx on it that prevented it from ever being accepted again. A pity, because it was about a curious party in a Dublin flat attended by a dozen people, including myself, all strangers to me, except for the thirteenth arrival – late because he was in fact a gatecrasher whom I had met once before – Patrick Kavanagh. When he entered, he looked around, didn't like what he saw, sat on the floor for a minute and then rose and shuffled out.

All the information I had recorded about manuscript submissions in these suddenly found pages led to the crunch question: how much had the fees totalled? Unfortunately, I couldn't be accurate – perhaps the mice-nibblers had known what best parts to devour – but the figure I assessed was between three hundred and three hundred and fifty pounds. It doesn't sound very much, not these days anyway, but that was too long ago to cause me present pain. The only writer, to the best of my knowledge, who disclosed in an autobiography how much his writing had earned him was

Anthony Trollope. His figure came to £68,939.17.6, but it covered thirty years from 1847 to 1879, and some forty-six novels and
tales. 'I look on the result,' he commented, 'as comfortable, but
not splendid.'

Perhaps I could have commented on my own results as rather
'uncomfortable' and worlds away from 'splendid', but once the
whole adventure was over, what I set my mind to was not the
financial result, but what the experience had taught me. It had
told me that I was neither a notable poet nor short story writer,
about either of which there was no gainsaying and so I closed the
book on it. Was I assailed by lasting, painful regrets? I don't know,
because it all happened too long ago to remember now how I felt
then. Who once said that an optimist is someone who knows how
bad the world is, a pessimist is still finding it out? It wasn't said by
me, but if I had been more worldly-wise at the time, the thought
would surely have been mine.

The unexpected recovery of my ancient manuscript record
also brought on a somewhat Proustian 'involuntary memory' associated with books. In my early teens, I and my two older brothers
were all avid readers, and having only a small bookcase in the sitting room where we and our parents spent our evenings, our constantly growing ranks of books were simply piled up on the floor
around the walls. To restore the room's appearance, our father
made for us a set of shelves, five feet wide and six feet high from
the ground. In next to no time our few hundred books filled a
great deal of space.

Unfortunately, a difficulty arose. Frequently my father's friends
would run their eyes over our book titles, now easily accessible,
and if some book attracted their special interest, my father would
always tell them to take it home and read it. Needless to say, some
were never returned, and my father never insulted a friend by
delivering a reminder. Eventually my brothers and I had to do
something about it. So we had a council-of-war, and one of us –
probably the oldest one – composed a couplet, printed it in cop-

perplate capitals on a neat, white card, and pinned the card on one of the higher shelves. It said:

> The benefits of friendship don't extend
> To wives or books, these borrow not, nor lend.

Visitors always read the notice, enjoyed it, some uproariously, but still borrowed a book, too many of whom forgot to return it. So something even more drastic had to be done. We added a word underneath the couplet. Just one word. And to my recollection, we never lost another book.

The word was
SHAKESPEARE.

Face To Face

When Aaron awoke next morning he was surprised to feel so at ease. Normally when he awakened his initial reaction was a recognisable touch of bad temper – though with whom could he be bad-tempered, apart from himself? God perhaps? Perhaps, though for a very long time he had tried not to get involved with that man. He always thought of God as a man, by which he meant the boss-man, the kind who so often makes a mess of things. But this morning he wasn't narky or worried. Then his memory – which habitually, like his age, did not wake up as early as he did himself – suddenly stirred and came back to life.

The call from the person at the newspaper office. That was it. She was to phone him later. And somehow he knew exactly what he was going to do about her. But how did he know he had made a decision? When did it happen? In his dreams? Could have been, he never remembered dreams unless his wife was in them, but no matter. The visit would be something new, something rare, and he didn't need to think any more about how he would deal with it. He already knew what course it would take. He hoped she'd phone when she said she'd phone. Unpunctuality always annoyed him.

As he made his breakfast coffee and toast, he checked that he had biscuits and cake in the cupboard. To a visitor – whether a chance one or not – food and drink had always been offered when his wife was alive. It was an old Jewish obligation – and an old

Irish one too – and it was some years since he had had the opportunity of fulfilling it. He didn't want to slip up on it now, so he put the cake and biscuits on a little table for her beside a comfortable chair. He'd need to soften her up in every possible way he could if she was the sort of person he might persuade of what he had in mind. If … if … if only. But he must keep calm. He was old enough and experienced enough to realise that nothing whatever might come of it.

She phoned on time. He didn't rush to answer. He didn't want her to think he had been waiting beside the phone. When she spoke his name, he spoke back with a friendly 'Good morning'. He was remembering to be pleasant this time, right from the beginning.

'If you're free now, come along. My address is –'

'I know where you are, Mr Cohen. I'll be with you in ten minutes. See you soon. Bye-bye.'

Aaron liked the sound of her voice. But was it too young? Nonsense. Women's voices always sounded young. Still, he hoped she'd be – what was it? – a bit mature?

When the doorbell rang he had a moment of panic when he realised he was wearing his *yarmulkah*. From habit he always wore it in the house, first thing every morning, but perhaps on this occasion he should have thought of it and thrown it aside. Steady, steady. Be yourself. I'm nearly ninety, amn't I?

'Mr Cohen?' she asked.

'Yes. It's me. I'm still here. Come in, you're welcome.'

'Thank you,' she said as she entered the sitting room. She stood for a moment and looked around. There was an electric fire, two bars lit, and she was glad of that. The air out had been cold and foggy. She took off her gloves and warmed her hands.

'Let me take your coat,' he said, and as he turned to put it in the hallway, she saw the little skull-cap on his head.

'Forgive me asking, but do you wear that on your head because of the cold?'

It clearly amused her, so Aaron didn't take it amiss.

'No, it's known as a *yarmulkah*, what orthodox Jews always wear indoors and in synagogue.'

'Why? And it's white, very attractive.'

'It's usually black, but I prefer white. Like your Pope's. Presuming, of course, that you're a Catholic.'

'Well, I was born a Catholic. But of course I was never given a choice, so now I make my own choices.'

'Sit down, do,' Aaron motioned to the chair, impressed by her having a mind of her own. That was promising, he thought. 'I'm afraid my memory is an old man's, so I haven't yet remembered your name. I'm sorry.'

'No fault,' as she sat down. 'It's Catherine. Catherine O'Driscoll.'

'Catherine, very attractive name. And I must add that as well as my memory being an old man's, so are my manners. So may I ask whether you're Miss O'Driscoll, or Miz, or Mrs.'

She smiled, rather cheekily. 'I don't think of myself as any of these, so do call me just Catherine.'

Aaron felt he'd been thrown, and deliberately so. He hadn't reckoned with this. He had felt certain he'd find out what he wanted to know about her without seeming inquisitive. He needed a moment to think.

'Would you like a cup of tea or coffee, Catherine?'

To make it would give him a chance to recover. She looked young, but how could he tell how old a female looked these days? With make-up they could be from twenty to forty or fifty. He should have thought about this beforehand. He wasn't near enough to see if she had any lines in her face, but even if there were, they could have been disguised, couldn't they? And he couldn't see if she was wearing a ring because one hand covered the other one.

'Tea, coffee?' he repeated.

'No thanks, Mr Cohen. I had coffee just before I left the office. I'd much rather sit and talk with you. And perhaps we could start

the interview. Would you mind if I use my little tape-recorder?'
She picked up her bag from the floor and opened it.

'Don't get out that thingamebob yet. I'd much prefer to talk
with you first, generally, about yourself. How long have you been
with the *Examiner*? Sorry, I know it's now the *Irish Examiner*, but
to me it has always been the *Cork Examiner*.'

Catherine smiled again. 'Well, I've been with them for almost
a year. A sort of reporter. A very inexperienced one. Not what I
was really interested in. But getting to do this interview is the first
kind of decent assignment I've been given.'

'Interviewing a ninety-year old crock doesn't sound much of
an assignment for you. There's nothing interesting at all in my
life.'

'Nonsense, Mr Cohen. You're the last Jew in Cork. That's not
only interesting, it's important.'

'It would be much more "important", as you call it, if you
waited until I reach a hundred. Now that would be something,
wouldn't it?'

'Then I'd do another interview with you then,' she said, with
her bright, perky laugh.

When did he last hear anyone laugh in this house? Except on
television. This girl's laugh was real, lively, welcome.

'Somehow, my girl, I can't see you being with the *Examiner* in
ten years' time.

'Why do you say that, Mr Cohen?'

'Well, you strike me as someone with too much intelligence,
and probably ambition too, to want to stay doing this kind of job
for much longer. Did you go to college? I bet you have some degree.'

She didn't reply immediately. She looked around the room, at
its sparse furnishings, two soft chairs – Mr Cohen occupying the
other one – a chest of drawers, one photograph on it, no flowers, a
television set, a radio, the phone, a standard lamp, and a small table
with only two chairs against the single window. Nothing else.

'I don't see any books, Mr Cohen. Do you not read?'

'Well, I read the *Examiner*,' he said with a smile.

'But no books.'

'Not very often. I don't buy any. Now and again I go to the public library. I sometimes read in the reference room. It's a change from sitting here alone. And you? Do you read?'

'Yes, I do read. I read a lot. I never went to college – which you asked me about. I couldn't afford to when … Well, I had to get a job, you know, the usual kind. Shop assistant. I had no particular qualifications. I didn't go out much because I wanted to save as much money as I could. To get away, somewhere else, make a life for myself. But … things happened.'

'Forgive me, Catherine, I didn't mean to pry. I'll be honest: all I wanted to find out was how old you are.'

'How old I am? But what difference does that make?'

'Simply that I didn't want to be interviewed by a youngster. I wouldn't be comfortable with a young girl. I never had a daughter and, being nearly ninety, I wanted you to be someone, well, mature, which I think you are, and intelligent, which I'm sure you are, as I said before, and reasonably experienced with life. I'm not offending you, am I?'

'No, you're not offending me. I'll level with you, Mr Cohen. I'm thirty, and I do have some experience of life. I was an orphan, I was never married but I did live with someone for a number of years, but he walked out on me. And I'm not, and never was, a mother. Is all that OK?'

'Yes, very OK.'

'Good. Then do I pass the test as a suitable interviewer?'

'Yes, I'm sure you do. But … Forgive me, please forgive me. I'm afraid I've got you here on false pretences.'

Catherine made no reply for some moments. Then, 'I can guess. You don't want to be interviewed. Isn't that it?'

'I'm sorry, really sorry. And I'm glad you've guessed it yourself. You're amazingly sharp.'

'But why didn't you tell me this morning on the phone? Why did you bring me out here on a wild goose chase?'

'I didn't tell you on the phone because I wanted to explain things to you.'

'What things?'

'Interviewing me would be pointless. My life has been almost completely uninteresting. Uninteresting to your readers, I mean.'

'But don't you think I might have the ability to present it in such a way that it would be interesting to our readers. Without distorting it, or inventing anything. And of course I'd show it to you before the editor sees it. Would that make you change your mind?'

Aaron hesitated. Then, 'No. And yes. Sort of.'

'Really, Mr Cohen, you'd almost make me laugh if you weren't so puzzling. Now come on, come clean. What are you up to?'

'What I'm up to, Catherine, is ... is this. As I told you, my own life has had nothing special in it. It's not that I'm trying to conceal anything. I'm the last Jew in Cork, and that's about the only distinction I can claim, if you can call it a distinction. So there's no story in me. The real story is between Cork's first Jews and its last Jews. It's a bit of history, Catherine, and a part of Cork's history too. Is it to be lost forever after more than a century's existence? I'm not superstitious, but only last night it came to me that as Cork's last Jew there's no one else to tell the story. And almost immediately I thought – at least hoped – that you might be a suitable person to write it down. I suppose it's my duty to try to tell it, or at least as much of it as I can. The trouble is that I don't even know how much I know of it myself, and at my age, much of what I might have known might by now be gone and forgotten. And to cap it all, I couldn't put it on paper, not in proper writing. My mind goes blank if I try to write. But I'm sure you can write or the editor wouldn't have given you the job of interviewing me. Tell him I refuse to be interviewed, but tell him what I've suggested. Instead of an empty interview of me for maybe half a page, you could write for the paper a whole week's instalments about Cork's Jewish life and people.'

'Mr Cohen, Mr Cohen, hold on,' Catherine interrupted. 'I imagine I'd be able to write an interview with a person, but writing about people, places, happenings, customs, religion, etcetera, etcetera – no matter how much you'd tell me, how could I write it properly? For something like that, one needs understanding, depth, colour, description, and I'm not a historian. What about places, buildings, things like that – even if you talked of them, I've never seen them. No, Mr Cohen, it's not on.'

Aaron looked at her, smiled and nodded.

'Catherine O'Driscoll, what you have just said proves that you'd be wasting your talent doing an interview. It proves you have in one moment expressed exactly what the story would need. All the places you would need to see, all the places where the Jews lived, worked, prayed, I could show you them, and I'm certain you could make them live again, even if some of them might have changed. If you tell your editor what I've told you, he'd be mad to say no, wouldn't he?'

Catherine rose from her chair and went over to the chest of drawers to examine the only photograph displayed on it. It was a wedding photograph, bride and groom, just the two, in black and white outside a building that had a Star of David cut into the masonry. The bride wore a simple, straight dress and carried a bouquet, the groom wore a dark suit, very old-fashioned, correct.

'You and your wife on your wedding, Mr Cohen?'

'Yes. That's my wife, Miriam.'

'When was it?'

'It was seventy years ago. She was eighteen.'

'She was beautiful, really beautiful.' Catherine turned to him. 'It's lucky for me today because the editor is away, so I don't have to tell him until tomorrow that we're not doing an interview. I'll have to tell him then, and I'll let you know.'

'And what about my suggestion, Catherine?'

'I'll have to think about it. It's a bit out of the blue and it's not something I could say yes to just like that. Besides, even if I do suggest it to him, he may not let me. Anyway we'll see.'

'Yes, we'll see. Thank you.'

'You too, Mr C.'

There was that smile again, the cheeky smile. They shook hands. She left.

God above, what does that man, Aaron Cohen, think he's up to? Doesn't he know I'm a Corkman myself, *and* a Jew? And Cork is *my* hometown. I said it, didn't I, that characters like that get out of control, think of mad things to do. So what sort of a *golem* have I created? The Talmud defined a *golem* as a brought-to-life, artificial, human figure; and one of the Grimm Brothers, Jakob, wrote that the Polish Jews were able to make him their servant; and what's more, Mary Shelley is supposed to have based Frankenstein on the *golem* legend. How foolish I was to say that I'd write a novel about Aaron, this last Jew in Cork, and backpack it on my second volume of autobiography, and now here he is like a *golem*, on top of *my* book and his hands around my neck. How am I going to get rid of him?

Perhaps that nice girl, Catherine O'Driscoll, will have enough sense to cook his goose. Perhaps.

The Jewish Santa Claus

Identity has to be self-discovered, and more often than not, that doesn't happen until one moves from home to a different place, circle, culture – or religion. For most people the change of circumstances doesn't occur in the years of childhood. For me, however, it did, when I went to a primary school in Cork and found that the pupils weren't Jewish. Yet the difference between me and them didn't arise from our different religious beliefs – which weren't even mentioned – it arose from Christmas.

When I first went to school I was also beginning to go to synagogue, not only on the Saturday Sabbath-day, but regularly on every Jewish festival. What a tally they made, what a tale each one told. Variety, colour, exoticism – every annual repetition was eagerly awaited.

Purim commemorated the story told in the Book of Esther about Haman, the Agagite – the first Hitler – who drew lots to discover the date on which he would destroy the Jews, and whenever his name is mentioned in the synagogue account, everyone present thumps as hard as possible on the front of his pew. Youngsters, like me, banged the loudest.

Rosh Ha-Shanah, the New Year festival, is the first of the Ten Days of Penitence during which one must repent of all sins committed in the previous year. The *shofar*, the ram's horn blown by the minister, leads on to the Tenth day, the Day of Atonement, in which one's judgement is sealed by God. One prays all day in the synagogue, and from the previous evening one has fasted so that for some twenty-six hours not a crumb of food or a drop of liquid may pass one's lips – even brushing one's teeth is forbidden. To take part in the fast, males must be thirteen years old, but I, out of bravado, accomplished it successfully a year earlier.

Among the many other festivals is *Hanukkah,* the Festival of Lights, which celebrates the victory of the Maccabees over Antiochus. On trying to rededicate the Temple by kindling the *menorah,* the candelabrum, the Maccabees could find only one sealed jar of oil, too little to last more than one night. By a miracle, however, it lasted eight nights until they could obtain new oil supplies. One of the most attractive rituals at home on each *Hanukkah* night is the lighting of the tiny coloured *menorah* candles – one on the first night, two on the second, and so on to the eighth. And as a youngster I knew of the modern prevalent custom to give Jewish children small presents on the final night so they wouldn't be disappointed at not getting presents as Christian children did at a similar season.

Which brought me to Christmas – and to Grand-Uncle Sopsa.

Grand-Uncle Sopsa was the only one of his kind, a Jewish *seanachie.* He learned about the *seanachie* in his youth, when he used to accompany his father on his weekly peddling trudges through the Irish country villages, and the image of the ancient Irish storyteller holding his audience in thrall around the winter fireside caught his fancy. The role suited him down to the ground, for he was a compulsive talker who never seemed to exhaust his fertile imagination. He fantasised embarrassingly in company, convincing everyone that he believed his own stories, as a result of which he gained the reputation of being harmlessly mad. Winter and summer he dressed in a sober pinstripe suit, boots polished to a sparkle, natty spats, and a grey Homburg hat. The hat never left his head, in keeping with the rule that an orthodox Jew should never leave his head uncovered, but while the other men of the community wore the traditional *yarmulkah* indoors, Grand-

Uncle Sopsa wore his hat. Once, accidentally, he happened to knock it off when he was bending down to tie his bootlaces. He was quite bald, and in that moment he looked a total stranger.

The secret ridicule of the grown-ups greatly frustrated him. They were never willing listeners, and he had no wife or family whose attention he could command. That left him either to talk to himself – which he did – or to take any opportunity he could to tell stories to youngsters. I took his stories as mere entertainment, little guessing that what he was doing was signposting the way into the real world I would very soon have to enter.

One winter, when I was still young enough to be inquisitive about Christmas and certainly envious of the Christmas presents schoolmates always got, Grand-Uncle Sopsa told me the truth about Santa Claus.

'Of course,' he said to me as the fire danced up the chimney and outside the window the early darkness hardened and grew cold, 'I'm sure you're too grown-up now to believe in Santa Claus, not that you ever did –'

I avoided his eyes, anxious to conceal the doubts that even yet might be lingering in my mind. We had nothing that could remotely compare with Christmas. There was the whole atmosphere of the season – the extra-busy streets, the rows of turkeys hanging like aeroplanes nose-diving into the ground, the festooned shop windows, the carol singers surrounded by knots of smiling pedestrians and not one saying that it was wrong to be singing out of doors. In the biggest store in Cork Santa Claus used to make a special two-week visit, but of course I was never taken to see him. Once I sneaked down to see what it was like. I didn't stay long. I found it too unbearable, listening to all those lucky children screaming with anticipation as they waited to whisper a few words into Santa's ear and exchange their shillings for a brightly wrapped box from his own hand. Each day at school in break time, it being too cold to go out, I sat dumbly drinking in their discussions of what each one was expecting to find in his stocking on Christ-

mas morning. That seemed the crowning bit of magic. The only
magic *we* had was the moment during the Passover *seder* when the
front door was opened for Elijah, the prophet, to come in and
drink the glass of wine that had stood waiting for him all evening.
But when the door was closed not a drop had ever vanished from
the glass, so what sort of magic was that? It certainly couldn't hold
a candle to stories I heard of how Santa Claus would come down
the chimney with his bulging sack, how you had to hang up your
stocking on the end of your bed the night before, how you had to
be sure to be asleep or he might not leave anything for you, and
then the heart-stopping miracle of waking up to find your presents there, new, sparkling, ready to be played with.

And the Christmas trees! Everywhere I went they were shining and winking at me in front windows from whose open curtains I found it impossible to avert my gaze. Behind them I often
caught sight of mantelpieces crammed with Christmas cards, so
many that it seemed the people who lived in the houses must
have known everyone in the city and had friends all over Ireland.
All over the world.

Of course it was to Santa Claus that my thoughts and dreams
so often returned. To me Santa Claus *was* Christmas. In my mind's
eye I saw him flying through the sky in his tinkling sleigh, cheer-
fully noting all the houses on his list. I was reminded of the ancient Israelites enslaved in Egypt, when the Lord, visiting the ten
plagues on Pharaoh and his cruel people, sent the Angel of Death
to slay all the Egyptian first-born but to pass over the houses of
the Children of Israel. Santa Claus was another angel who had to
pass over the houses of the Children of Israel, but I yearned for it
to be otherwise. And the more I yearned, the more guilty I felt.
So when Grand-Uncle Sopsa said that he would tell me the truth
about Santa Claus, I hoped that, if what he was going to reveal
did not salve my conscience, it might at least ease my regrets.

'Now,' he commenced, 'you never knew a boy named Yankel
Birzansky. It was before you were born and the Birzanskys don't

live here any more. Yankel had no brothers or sisters, but he had loving parents whose greatest wish was to see him grow up into a good, strong, clever boy. Good Yankel was, though, no better I'm sure than you.' Grand-Uncle Sopsa smiled innocently, making me feel that he knew I could be a bit of a devil at times, but a harmless one. 'And strong,' he went on, 'my goodness, Yankel was certainly big and strong. Would you believe when he was eight, people who didn't know him thought he was twelve already. Good – strong – clever. Clever? Well, so-so. Not stupid, but not a genius. Too much of a dreamer. That worried his father, Shlomo Birzansky, because dreamers don't get very far in life. Shlomo had to work hard to make a living. "Where would we be," he said to his wife, Rachel, "if I were a dreamer?" And so Shlomo thought a lot about how to bring his son down to earth.

'Christmas, of course, meant nothing to Shlomo and Rachel. Why should it! They were good Jews, and Christmas was a Christian festival. Yankel was a good Jewish boy too – he had been going to *cheder* since he was six, he could read his Hebrew prayerbook, and already he was able to recite the *Kiddush* after his father at the commencement of the Sabbath every Friday night. But come December, all he could talk about was Christmas!'

At this I squirmed a bit in my seat. I knew exactly how Yankel Birzansky had felt.

'Now where had Yankel heard so much about Christmas?' Grand-Uncle Sopsa asked. (I knew the answer to that too.) 'In school of course, where I'm sure you hear about Christmas every year also. But Yankel wasn't like you. As I told you, he was a dreamer, and all the wonderful stories about Christmas – especially about Santa Claus – made him wish – well, not exactly that he had been a Christian, but that, even though he was a Jew, Santa Claus might be able to come down his chimney just once.'

More squirming from me. How different had I been from Yankel Birzansky, I asked myself.

'"What will we do with him, Rachel?" Shlomo appealed.

"What will become of our son? How can we make him realise that he can't dream his way through life? All this talk about Christmas and Santa Claus ..."

'Rachel didn't share her husband's worries. Yankel would surely grow out of his childish dreams. Another year or two and Christmas and Santa Claus would mean nothing to him. Shlomo was a good man but he expected too much too soon. Time enough to be strict with their son. He was still only a big baby.'

Grand-Uncle Sopsa shrugged, as if to let me know that he neither agreed nor disagreed with Rachel Birzansky. But I guessed that Shlomo hadn't agreed with his wife, and I was right.

'Shlomo looked at his "big baby" and shook his head. A few years time might be too late. Already nature had developed his body but it hadn't developed his mind. His parents would have to do that. Shlomo looked again at his son and made his decision. It was time to act.

"'My son," he said, one very cold day a week before Christmas when the skies were dark and Yankel was gazing out the window at the falling snow, "I have a surprise for you."

'Yankel looked up in wonderment. Or perhaps I should say that he looked down in wonderment, for already he was bigger than his father.'

I laughed uproariously. Grand-Uncle Sopsa's joke helped break the tension of waiting to hear what Shlomo Birzansky was going to do.

"'A surprise?" Yankel said. "What is it, *Tata?*"

'Rachel Birzansky said nothing. She wasn't happy with her husband's plan.

"'This year, Yankel," Shlomo said, and he paused a moment to make his announcement more dramatic, "this year we are going to celebrate Christmas."

'Yankel looked at his father but didn't utter a word. He thought he must not have heard properly or else that his father had suddenly lost his senses.

'Shlomo Birzansky was disappointed. He had expected shouts of joy, wild excitement, perhaps even a little dance, but instead all he got was silence and a puzzled stare.

'"Christmas," he repeated, "you know what Christmas is. You talk enough about it. Well, we're going to have Christmas this year, in this house, and you can do all the things that your Christian schoolfriends do at Christmas. What do you say to that?"

'"But *Tata* …" was all Yankel could say.

'"I know what you're thinking," his father told him. "You are thinking Christmas is a Christian festival, so how can a Jew observe it?"

'Yankel nodded.

'"Why not?" Shlomo continued. "Nothing in the five Books of Moses says we can't celebrate Christmas. It's supposed to be a season of goodwill. Well, Abraham, Isaac, Jacob, Moses – they were all men of goodwill. Can a good Jew not join in such a celebration?"

'"You mean Santa Claus would be able to come down our chimney?" Yankel asked doubtfully.

'"How else would he bring your presents?"

'"Presents!" Yankel's thoughts were beginning to race with visions of the wonderful toys he would get.

'"You will write Santa Claus a letter," Shlomo declared, "just as all your schoolfriends do, telling him what presents you want – only remember, don't be greedy, he has millions of other children to consider. We'll have a Christmas tree, and on Christmas Eve you'll hang up your stocking before you go to bed, and while you're asleep, Santa Claus will come. Yes?"

'Yankel looked towards his mother for confirmation. He still could not believe it. Something would go wrong or his father would change his mind. Rachel looked back at him. There were tears in her eyes. He thought they must be tears of happiness for his good fortune.

'He got busy immediately. Almost crying with anticipation

and excitement he got pen and ink, tore a clear white page from his school jotter, and sat down with his father to write his letter to Santa Claus.

'It turned out that it wasn't as easy a letter to write as he had imagined. There were so many toys and games he wanted to have. That was the difficulty – choosing between them, because he couldn't ask for them all.'

I nodded. I understood how difficult his problem was – not that I would have minded having such a problem myself.

'At last, with his father's help, he decided on three presents, three presents so wonderful, so alluring, that never in his wildest dreams had he seen himself as one day possessing them. They were a Hornby train set complete with passenger carriages, Pullman cars, wagons, stations, bridges, viaducts, signals, and water tanks; a Number Seven Meccano set; and a fountain pen to make him the envy of every boy in the class. He blotted the letter carefully, put it in an envelope, addressed it, and gave it to his father to post. Shlomo Birzansky solemnly put the letter in his pocket and said he would post it that very day. Rachel stood by. She said nothing. She felt sad, but she still said nothing.

'When Shlomo returned from his store that evening, Yankel ran up to him excitedly to ask if his letter had been posted, but when he saw what his father had brought home he could only stand dumbly and gaze in awe. A Christmas tree! A real, magical, spell-binding Christmas tree! And a box of fairy lights, all colours of the rainbow, to make it sparkle and glow just the same as all the other Christmas trees in the road! Yankel insisted that they put it up immediately, without even waiting until they had their tea, so he and his father set to work and in no time at all the tree was standing in all its glory, its lights shining and winking on the outstretched branches. But there was one thing missing. Yankel and his father looked at each other. Both of them knew what it was.

'"But we can't put an angel on top," Shlomo said. "Jews don't have angels."

'"Some trees have stars, *Tata*," Yankel answered. "Couldn't we just have a star?"

'Shlomo's eyes lit up, almost as brightly as the sparkling lights. A star! The very thing!

'Quickly he cut out a star from a big piece of card, coloured it blue and white, the Jewish colours, and pinned it proudly to the top of the tree.

'"There," he said, stepping back to admire his work, "*Magen Dovid*, the Star of David, the emblem of the Jews. Now that's *really* a Jewish Christmas tree!"

'Yankel laughed and laughed. His mother saw his joy and her heart was heavy.

'Over the next few days Yankel's excitement kept growing until by the time Christmas Eve arrived he couldn't sit still for a single moment. But for Rachel it was otherwise. With Shlomo out at work all day, it was to her that her son brought all his questions. She tried her best to explain what Christmas was supposed to mean. But when he asked about Santa Claus – as he increasingly did – she was lost for answers. What could she say to him when he wondered where Santa Claus lived, when he said that surely it must be impossible to ride through the skies behind a team of reindeer, when he protested that even if Santa Claus *could* succeed in making such a miraculous journey, how in the world could he manage to come down a narrow chimney with a bulging sack on his back? Wouldn't he get stuck? And there was the question he kept coming back to, the one that completely defeated him – and completely defeated all Rachel's attempts to explain away: how could three stores – *three* stores – in the same city possibly have Santa Claus visit them *all at the same time?*

'She was glad when Christmas Eve came – glad because soon the whole business would be finished with. She expected that Christmas Day, and the few days afterwards, would bring her a greater trial, but at least it would be the sort of trial a mother was used to – that of comforting her heart-broken child when one of his most precious dreams has been shattered.'

At this point Grand-Uncle Sopsa left me for a moment to step into the kitchen for a drink of water, but I was so spellbound by the story of Yankel Birzansky and Santa Claus that I didn't say a word or move a muscle when he was gone. When he returned, he settled himself, and then went on.

'Yankel was allowed to stay up late on the big night – anyway he was much too excited for bed, and Shlomo wanted to make sure his son would not stay awake too long but would quickly fall into a heavy sleep. He helped him to hang up his stocking, explaining that of course the big presents wouldn't fit in but that Santa would leave them at the foot of the bed and probably leave a small, special gift in the stocking. Then Rachel said goodnight to her son, holding him close to her bosom until he had to struggle to free himself so that he could lie back, bury his head in his pillow, and have the great adventure begin. Together his parents left the room, closing the door quietly behind them.

'Mr and Mrs Birzansky sat side by side in their kitchen for the next few hours, not speaking. Shlomo knew how much his wife disapproved of what he was doing but he told himself that sometimes a parent has to be cruel to be kind. Rachel gazed for a long time at the fairy lights winking on the Christmas tree until they appeared to be mocking her. She got up and switched them off. There had never been Christmas in the Birzansky home and there never would be – least of all for her son.

'Her action seemed to awaken Shlomo and remind him of what he had to do. She watched him take a small white card from his wallet and write something on it. She did not have to read what he had written. She knew what it was: *Santa Claus does not exist.*

'"It is time," he said. "He should be well asleep by now."

'She nodded. They both rose. She followed him to her son's bedroom.

'Soundlessly Shlomo Birzansky opened the door a few inches

and peeped in. In the darkness he could just make out a humped figure in the bed. It was quite motionless. Yankel was fast asleep.'

Grand-Uncle Sopsa paused. I held my breath.

'Slowly Shlomo pushed the door open wide enough for him to creep into the room. His wife did not follow him. She waited out-side, her back to the door, her eyes closed tight to stifle her sorrow.

'Like a ghost, Shlomo tiptoed across the floor towards the end of Yankel's bed. He had to grope along it to find the stocking hanging there, limp and empty. Into it he dropped his card: *Santa Claus does not exist*. Then, as silently as he had come, he turned and tiptoed back towards the door.

'He had just reached the threshold when suddenly some huge object rose up from behind the door and threw itself at him. With a crash Shlomo was knocked flying. His elbow hit the floor and his head hit the wall so hard that he thought it would burst open. "I've got him, I've got him," the object cried, "I've caught Santa Claus."

'"Help! Help! I'm murdered!" Shlomo shrieked as Rachel Bir-zansky rushed in and switched on the light. She found her hus-band stretched on the ground, trying to hold his reeling head in his hands and rub his elbow at the same time. Beside him was her son. In the bed the pillow had been bundled up under the covers to look like a sleeping figure.

'"Yankel, Yankel," Rachel cried, "it's not Santa Claus. It's your father."

'"I know," Yankel laughed. "I knew all the time."

'Shlomo Birzansky stopped nursing his wounds and stared at his son. "You knew?"

'"Of course I knew. I've known for years."

'"How did you find out?" his father asked.

'"The boys at school told me. They know it's their fathers put the presents in their stockings but they pretend it's Santa Claus so as to keep getting presents every Christmas."

'Yankel turned to look for the presents he believed his father had brought. Seeing no Hornby train set, no box of Meccano, he went to the hanging stocking and peered into it. He took out the card nestling inside and read it. Silently he turned to his parents, his eyes clouded with disappointment, his lip quivering.

'Rachel had helped her husband to his feet and they both stood looking at their son. He was doing his best to keep back his tears. Shlomo was still rubbing his head, trying to soothe his pain.

'"Come," Rachel said, taking his arm. "It's late and Yankel must get some sleep. I'll put some lint on your elbow and when you lie down you'll feel much better."

'She pushed Shlomo out of the room, but before closing the door she slipped a hand into her apron pocket and drew from it a sparkling silver fountain pen. She held it out to Yankel. In an instant the tears were banished and his eyes lit up with joy. A fountain pen! Now he'd be the only boy in his class with a fountain pen. He took it in his hands and kissed his mother.

'"I hope *Tata* will be all right," he said. "I hope I didn't hurt him."

'"Only his pride, Yankel, only his pride," she whispered. "But he'll get over it."

'Later, when husband and wife were lying together in bed, Rachel said, "You see, my man, our son isn't stupid. He isn't such a dreamer after all."

'"You mean because he knew about Santa Claus? Because he was only pretending to believe in him?"

'"Not only that, wise one. Didn't you notice that he waited until you had put something in his stocking before knocking you down. Clever boy! He wasn't going to attack Santa Claus until *after* he'd had a chance to deliver his presents."

'In the darkness Shlomo Birzansky thought about what his wife had said. After a while he smiled happily to himself and turned on his side to go to sleep. His elbow no longer ached, his head had stopped throbbing, and perhaps his son would turn out to be as clever as his father after all!'

Almost a month after Grand-Uncle Sopsa's story about the Bir-zanskys and Santa Claus, he sent for me. I hadn't seen him since then because he had been ill, very ill. When I went to his room he was sitting in a chair by his bed. He looked so different – instead of the pinstripe suit he was in pyjamas and a dressing-gown, instead of the sparkling boots and spats his feet were in carpet slippers. But the familiar grey Homburg was still on his head and to some extent that helped offset the almost frightening pallor of his skin.

'*Dovidil*,' he said, using the pet version of my Hebrew name, something he had never used before, and which even my parents had already stopped calling me.

'*Dovidil*,' he repeated, 'I just wanted the chance to thank you for listening to that story about Christmas. It's a true story, one that really happened, not like the other ones I just make up – used to make up. I never told it to anyone except you. I hope you will always remember it and me.'

He smiled shyly, and the intimacy of the smile, the quite deliberate revelation in his admission about all the stories he had told in his life – both to children and to adults – shocked me out of my own self-absorption and helped me to understand and learn from Grand-Uncle Sopsa's wisdom and love. The coming to an end of that special link marked the beginning of my growing up.

He died the next day.

Lives on an Ocean Wave

I s there room for a book on the history of book launching? Publishers, to keep in business, need a never-ending succession of histories about everything and anything, no matter how arcane or bizarre. But to research the story of book launching may be almost an impossible, and certainly a lifelong task. When was the first one? Where did it take place? What was the name of the book and writer, and its publisher? And who did the honours? Was the book one of fiction? Likely, but by no means certain. Poetry? Unlikely. And presumably a dramatist can be said to have been launched if his or her play had been produced, whether or not the writer had attended the first performance.

The whole topic of book launching occurred to me not many years ago when I was asked to launch a particular book. The request set me wondering what was the first launch of a book by an Irish writer. I had no idea – does anyone know? – and I certainly didn't intend to follow up my own curiosity. What more concerned me, however, was the innate problem of what I should say in my launch address. I shouldn't rattle on for too long, because it was to see the writer and his or her book that the audience had come. But exactly what, and how much could I reveal about the book? I had, of course, read it, but I had to keep in mind that the audience hadn't. So while briefly outlining the book's absorbing themes and characters, and mentioning the fascination and delight of the writer's style, I had to take care not to spoil the audience's anticipation of the main event, i.e. the writer's expected address.

Somehow I wasn't enamoured of coming up with such a straightforward, fairly run-of-the-mill speech. It's much easier to launch a boat than to launch a book. To launch a boat, all you have to do is smash a bottle on its hull and say 'I name you xyz', but I could hardly smash a bottle on the spine of the book I was launching. However, I realised that I was in the lucky situation of being able to sidestep telling the audience about the innards of the book, or its story, or its characters, by using something I happened to be privy to: the author's creative traumas and his original manuscript's ever-surfacing troubles. The book was *At Swim, Two Boys* by Jamie O'Neill, but the story of my fortuitous discovery of the writer's existence dates back to April 1998.

In that month I made one of my regular visits to Rathmines Public Library which has a special set of bookshelves. Special to me at least because the short story has always been my obsession, and anthologies of such graced these shelves. I spotted one I hadn't seen before, one of the 'Winter's Tales' series under the Constable imprint. I pulled it out and ran my eye over the contents list to see if it had any Irish writers. Among them was the name, Jamie O'Neill, completely unknown to me. Surely he had to be Irish. I turned to the biographical notes and learned that he had been educated at Presentation College, Glasthule. That was enough for me. By an amazing coincidence, just on the same day I read in the current copy of *Books Ireland* that a novel by Jamie O'Neill was forthcoming. I asked in the bookshops if they had anything by this Irish writer. They had never heard of him. So without further delay I wrote to Jamie, c/o Constable, told him about the annual Irish short story anthology I was editing for the London publishers, Phoenix, and asked him if he had any unpublished stories. His quick reply said *I am in the middle of a much-delayed novel at the moment but I do have a 'short' short story hanging about and nearly finished. I'm not too sure about it but I'd be pleased to have*

*your opinion. Could you let me know what submission date you have
in mind?* I replied immediately that I was keenly looking forward
to the story; his response followed within a month. I think the
letter provides a valuable insight into the writer, and something,
too, that takes you behind the novel he was working on. He
wrote:

*Thank you for your letter. I'm now sending you the short story I men-
tioned earlier. Called 'Nights of Rhodes'. It's very short and not much
of a story: altogether rather light, I'm afraid. At one time I had thought
to delve deeper: explore who this boy is, why he's in Rhodes, what he's
running from, how he prospers (if he does). But I found I kind of liked
its looseness. What tension there is comes from the characterless boy
commented on by an older, ironical authorial voice. A kind of third person cloaking a first person narrative. Anyway, there it is. I'm pleased
with it. I would very much like to appear in your anthology (to be published at all in Ireland would be a treat) but I quite understand if it
doesn't reach your expectations …*

*You asked about my novel. Well, unfortunately it is the same as
was due for publication last year. Desperate, I agree. But I have a very
considerate publisher …* – [incidentally, this was not the present
publisher] … *and kind heart or force of circumstances, he's leaving me
finish it in my own good time. It's currently called 'At Swim Two Boys'
– catchy yes. It's set in Dun Laoghaire in 1915–16. Kingstown, I should
say. The two boys of the title plan to swim, politics permitting, from
the Forty Foot to the Muglins on Easter Sunday you know when. I've
never had to read so many books in my life and I wish to God I'd taken
history instead of French at Pres, Glasthule.*

*Anyway, the reason I'm going in to all this is that I find myself
stranded in London with ne'er an Irish friend to speak of. All those who
came over with me have returned home – not that they were ever much
use: the bookies was the closest they got to literature. I feel myself lost
inside of my novel and I was wondering if you might know of anyone
half-willing to read the half of it. I have the need of some outside ear,*

an Irish ear that might get the jokes and references and (the ear now having a voice) would tell was there any point my continuing. I've been at the book for some years now but I have a million ideas milling about my head and I'd far rather be getting on with them if the novel is, as I deeply fear, a non-starter. Would you know of such a person? Had you the time yourself and you were willing to spare it I would be truly grateful ... Thanks once again for the interest you have shown. Yours with twisted fingers.

Jamie O'Neill.

I replied on 2 June:

Thank you. I think 'Nights of Rhodes' is splendid – and a very impressive introduction to your work for Irish readers. Short? No perfect story is short or long – it has as many or as few words as it needs. And what words! The individuality of style, the authorial voice, the evocation of atmosphere, the bull's-eye descriptions, the rising off the page of your wandering nameless Dubliner – all is a huge success. I'm delighted to have this distinguished story ... and I'll use it next year ...

Your novel in progress sounds intriguing and of course I'd be happy – honoured – to read as much as you've written of it ...

Jamie's next letter said:

I got your letter, and indeed it was such a good letter, so bright and promising, that I have been this age replying to it. I wanted to send you some chapters of my novel to read and, allowing July for a little revising, I locked the door of my dungeon and have been scribbling the daylights out of me since. To small avail unfortunately ... I should love to meet if you do come to London. You will not be surprised to learn I have a day job – or rather, a night job: my hours are irregular, but if you could give me some notice, I'm sure something might be arranged. (Reading back over this, I see I am writing in a rather stilted style: the character I'm concentrating on at the moment speaks like this, or better,

he thinks like this. Amusing how they poke their noses into everything,
these people.) I do hope your offer still stands to read some of my chap-
ters. I have them nearly in a presentable form. And forgive me for not
replying sooner. Though it was rude, it was not rudeness but apprecia-
tion that delayed me.

Of course I was anxiously awaiting the promised chapters and
when Jamie's next letter came, dated 15 October, it commenced:

At last I have got my chapters into some kind of order. I'm sending them
to you under separate cover ... but I thought it only fair to give you
some warning that a rather big package may be expected. It's more than
300 pages. I do hope this isn't an imposition. Take your time reading
them.

Any ideas or suggestions you have would be hugely appreciated. I
gauge there to be another 200 pages to go. Would the story hold up for
that length? Is it interesting to an Irish reader? Is there a sense of the
past in it? I have a slippery suspicion I might be writing two novels here
instead of one. Do the themes meld at all? Some parts, I know them so
well now, reading them is like saying a prayer – the words have been
separated from their intention. I can no longer judge if they are appro-
priate even.

My publisher is starting to put the skids under me. Apparently I'm
to be in next spring's catalogue come what may. Time is running out
for them two boys if ever they're to swim to that island.

My reaction to the 300 odd pages was such that I decided to go
over to London and meet Jamie. I did so, and I gave him my
honest opinion of what I had read. I was convinced at that point
that he was well into something exceptionally special. He next
wrote to me on 16 December as follows:

I have been hoping to write to you for months now, but these things do
come so slowly to me. I don't suppose I shall ever be a man of letters.

*But I wanted to thank you for all the encouragement you have
given to me in my writing. I felt such a host of pride after our meeting
in London it was a blood infusion from the high Alps sanatorium.
Needless to say, I am speeding through the second half of my novel at
the sleepless rate of a winter tortoise.*

On New Year's Eve, 1998, I wrote to Jamie to let him know that
I was delighted to learn he was continuing to make headway with
the novel, but well into 1999 what he wrote was: *Alas, it doesn't
seem to be going at all this weather. Something to do with the chassis,
or it might be the brakes.* Also, he wasn't sure what the position was
with the publisher who held his rights, and he asked me would I
send him the name of the agent at Curtis Brown whom I had mentioned when we met in London, just in case his contract should
fall through. I replied that in such an eventuality I'd be happy to
recommend his novel to Giles Gordon in Curtis Brown, or Jamie
could send it to him himself if that should be his preference.

A month later I dropped him a line to find out how he was
and how the novel was progressing. On 24 November this is what
he wrote:

*At last I can write with good news. I've managed to buy back my
contract from my publisher! You can scarcely imagine my relief ... I'm
on the second last chapter now. I hope to have it finished by Christmas,
even Christmas this year! You know, I've had to turn my life round. I
sleep during the day and work the night through. It's a wonderful feeling
to see new pages coming through. You think you can't do it any more,
only correct previous drafts. But no, there they come again, floating out
of the printer. I'm always surprised how chapters begin just about where
you begin them. If I started a chapter the day before or after, would it
begin somewhere altogether different? And where would it end? I don't
know ... So I'll say this: I'm thinking about my next novel, pleasantly
working things out while I close my eyes in bed. Surely I'll see you soon
in Dublin.*

I replied a few weeks later and phoned him in July 2000, and at last, dated 6 September, came the following:

I hope you'll remember some time ago I sent you an early draft of a novel I was writing ... Well, I'm sending you now the manuscript of my novel, 'At Swim Two Boys', finished at long last. Finished, least-ways, as good as I can get it. I'm not too happy with the beginning and I'm not too happy with the end, and the title is only asking for trouble – but the middle parts I believe are good enough ... Honestly, I had hoped to keep from sending the ms till October, but the longer I have it round me, the more fiddling changes I make and the less satisfied I become and the more hopeless I feel. Would you pardon me thrusting it upon you this way?

Would you believe it's ten years since I started this story? ... I was writing away, my characters were getting on with it: one of them was roaming up O'Connell Street, when suddenly I remembered it wasn't called O'Connell Street then but Sackville Street – you might remember the novel is set in 1915. Well, what else did I not know of the period? Answer there came: nearly everything. What were my characters wearing? Which newspapers did they read? The sound, motion of a tram? Those studs I remember my grandfather had on his dressing table, what were they for? I hadn't the faintest. In a film, you see, there would be wardrobe people and set designers to deal with the period details: with a novel you are of course on your own. So that's when my researches began. I don't believe I've read a book since that moment which didn't have some bearing on the period, some detail, a word even, that without it, the other 180,000 words must infallibly sink ...

... it's odd the way these things go: it's not the reader you need to convince but yourself. When I was sure I was comfortable with some aspect – street lighting for instance – I was happy to write nothing about it. After all, who walks along a street noticing the lighting? But I need to be sure I knew enough in order to leave any of it out.

It's over, thank God, though I can scarcely persuade myself of it. These people that I ate, drank and slept with these past ten years, they're on their own now, and they must try to make their way in the world without me scribbling and scratching behind them. I don't feel an ounce of joy: relief maybe, and sadness a bit. I'm already a bit lonely without them.

I look forward to hearing from you. If you can't help me get the ms placed, frankly I'm at a loss what to do. I'll be like Molly Keane with a drawer-full of pages nobody ever read.

My reply went to Jamie on 24 September:

Dear Jamie, Neither you, nor certainly I, could have expected that I'd be writing you about your novel so quickly. But I finished it during last week. ... I don't want to go into a long disquisition about it at this stage because I want to parcel it up and send it tomorrow to Giles Gordon of Curtis Brown. But this much I must say: for me it is one of the very best novels by an Irish writer – no, dammit, by any writer – that I've read for a long, long time. It has tremendous originality both of style and content, transfixing characters, constant control, descriptive passages that one can actually see, relationships soaked with such understanding, wisdom and sympathy that only a master writer could deliver. But we can talk about it when you come over ...

Whether or which, it's a tremendous achievement and it gave me such pleasure to read. I found it almost unbearably moving. Well done, and thanks.

Jamie's reply was:

I want to thank you so very much for the letter you sent me. It was what every writer must hope to read about his writing. I think everyone of us should receive such a letter, at least once in a career. It made me feel that my book, which was a jungle of phrases and ideas, had really taken shape ... whatever about its being published, I feel I have a book written at long last.

The next letter to Jamie was from Giles Gordon, dated 12 October, and full of praise and advice, and within a matter of weeks Giles had sold *At Swim Two Boys* to the distinguished publishers, Simon & Schuster.

That was the end of the manuscript and the beginning of the book.

The writer acknowledges and thanks Jamie O'Neill for permission to include in this chapter correspondence that passed between them.

One and One Makes ...?

Suddenly, in the middle of the night, Aaron woke me up. Had I been dreaming about him? Perhaps, but my mind was still too dream-dulled to know if I had or hadn't been.

'What's wrong with you?' I asked him. 'What are you worrying about?'

'You're asking *me*!' he came back. 'What sort of a *chacham* are you? You're supposed to be the wise man, the writer. If *you* don't know what's worrying me, how can *I* know?'

By now I was properly awake and guessed that he must indeed have been pacing up and down in my dreams. So I closed my eyes and gave him my attention.

'She hasn't got in touch with you again,' I said. 'How long has it been?'

'Two days. Her editor was to be back by yesterday, so she must have told him about what I suggested. She might get back to me tomorrow. Today, I mean. Might she?'

'Yes, Aaron, but give her a chance. Don't be in such a hurry. I'd say Catherine O'Driscoll *might* get back to you today. Now let us both go back to sleep. If I don't get a proper night's sleep, how do you expect me to think properly? So *shluf*, Aaron. Sleep, old man, sleep.'

That quietened him, but I didn't go back to sleep immediately because I heard him mumbling away in the way that an old man like him who doesn't need sleep does. He needs to know what's worrying him. 'How can I know?' he was muttering. 'How can I know?'

'Oh, bugger it,' I muttered myself. 'How can *I* know if I'm too tired to think?'

Not surprisingly, by now I was awake enough to work out what Aaron's problem was, so I went over it bit by bit. It was something in the back of his mind that he couldn't face – not yet anyway. He had more or less refused to let Catherine O'Driscoll interview him for his ninetieth birthday, and instead he had suggested his sudden idea that she should do a number of articles for the *Examiner*, a sort of history of the Cork Jews. Much better than an interview, he claimed. Something the *Examiner* editor would surely go along with. His readers would lap it up – Jews are always news, good, bad or indifferent.

Naturally Catherine had immediately and sensibly pointed out to him that she couldn't possibly tackle such a job she knew nothing whatever about but, toning down all her difficulties, he explained that he'd tell her as much as he knew or could remember about the history of the Cork Jews and he'd show her all the relevant places she'd need to see. He'd have to tell it to her because he couldn't write it himself. 'My mind goes blank if I try to write', he'd said.

Aaron, Aaron, you're not going to pull the wool over *my* eyes. If she agrees to your idea, then you'd have fooled her into doing it, wouldn't you? You could write it yourself if you wanted to. Maybe not as well as she would, but well enough. So why are you leading her up the garden path, Aaron?

I went back to sleep, confident that I'd wake up with the answer. And I did. Loneliness. That was the answer, Aaron's loneliness. Living alone, no old friends, the only Jew still alive in Cork, and ninety just around the corner. Every few days he'd go out to buy food, sometimes a newspaper – though often he didn't bother to read it – go to the library for a few books. He had told Catherine that he read only in the reference room, but the books he borrowed were probably in his bedroom and he was only slinging her a line. He was secretive. No, not really secretive. Not even uncommunicative. Just holding back. Very old men, with no company, can gradually grow silent. Catherine had looked at his wedding photograph – the only photograph in the room – and he told her that his bride was eighteen and the wedding was seventy years ago. That was the only thing he mentioned about his own life. Beyond that he offered nothing, so Catherine asked nothing. Perhaps she was remembering he had said that as an old man, he believed in good manners, so she was careful not to be inquisitive. But if she had asked, would he have replied? There was only the wedding photograph on the sideboard. That was the question. And there, too, was the answer: not a picture of a son or sons; not a picture of a daughter or daughters. That's how I tumbled to it, to what had been worrying Aaron at the back of his mind. When Catherine, out of the blue, had asked to interview him, he hadn't known what to say, but he certainly didn't want to be interviewed by a youngster. If he wanted anyone, it would have to be a female, grown-up, intelligent and reasonably mature. Someone he could talk to. But what use would a one-off interview be. He might have plenty of time but he couldn't be bothered wasting any of it on that. It would be more or less question and answer, dry, formal, an hour or so, hello and goodbye. And no matter how many people in Cork might read it, he wouldn't know one of them. He'd have to take the phone off the hook because if any of them looked up his number in the book to phone him and tell him what they thought of it, he didn't want to know, he didn't want to be reminded how old he was, how much time he might or might not have left. That was what gave him the idea of the series of articles. If only she'd take it on … if only. He'd see a good deal of her, have a chance to get to know her, and she to know him. He had no children, had never been blessed to have the chance of being a father. He was afraid to say it even to himself but it kept spinning around in his mind. After all this time, in his last years, maybe last weeks, maybe even only days, not a single friend. Catherine O'Driscoll could be a friend. A good friend. If only she'd write these articles. If only she'd say yes. Oh, if only ...

OK Aaron, OK old man. It's up to me, isn't it?

All the Fun of the Games

A Proust-like involuntary memory only recently flew into my mind after having been planted there by my father about seventy years ago. He once, just once, told me that in his youth he had ridden in bicycle races. He never mentioned it again, or if he did, I've forgotten it. Did he also add that at that time the bicycle tyres were solid? If so, I've forgotten that too.

I never in all my life saw him ride a bike. There was never one in our home, except on the odd occasion one of my brothers might have had a brief loan of a friend's. Just as I had too. But one thing I'm certain of is that my father never won a race. If he had, he'd have told me, and that's surely something I'd not have forgotten. The only bicycle both of us together ever watched moving was the bizarre, *sui generis* progress of our neighbour, Mr Dennehy. Mr Dennehy cycled to work every morning and cycled home every late afternoon. Our belief is that he never really got into work, wherever it was, because immediately he'd have reached it, he'd have needed to turn around and cycle home. My father said that if his speed was just one mile an hour less than it was, his bicycle would have stopped and Mr Dennehy would have fallen off.

The one other sport – if I can call it a sport – that my father actually played was billiards. Not that I ever saw him perform, because I was much too young to be taken, and anyway he gave it up quickly. He used to go with one of his brothers-in-law, and I remember that the billiard hall was at the top of Patrick Street, just opposite the statue of Father Mathew. Poor Father Mathew, I used think, he was never able to jump down off his plinth, hop across into the billiard hall and take up a cue. Billiards, of course, lost its public appeal a long time ago, snooker becoming a major success on television. I've never held a cue myself, but the variety of shots it calls for and the spectacular brilliance of the leading players always hypnotise me. For an inveterate, but ageing TV sports viewer, soccer and rugby, Gaelic football and hurling with their speed, brawn and physical body-to-body challenges are one's most dangerous blood-stirrer, but then there's always the slow waltz of cricket and golf to calm the pulse.

Looking back now, however, I can recline in my armchair and recall the best – no, the greatest days of my life. I wasn't at the Los Angeles Olympic Games and I missed out on the Moscow ones too, and also the 1976 games in Montreal. Oh, I know if you look up the very old newspapers – and you know what's always said about them, that you can't believe a word they say – they'll tell you *their* version of the 1936 Olympic Games, but I clearly re-member, as if it was only yesterday, that the 1936 Olympic Games were held in Ireland in the back garden of my home in Cork.

I suppose that back garden wasn't more than thirty feet long and ten feet wide, bounded by kitchen windows and living room windows and glasshouse windows and high brick walls that divid-ed it from the neighbours – and it hadn't even any grass on it. But there wasn't an event, track or field, in the whole Olympic pro-gramme that it didn't accommodate.

Of course I was lucky that that particular year happened to be an Olympic Games year. I was really in my prime then – physi-cally, emotionally and psychologically packed tight with the brand of fantastic enthusiasm vital to enable me to go in there and win. Four years earlier I still was not much more than a child – four years later I was into my teens and beginning to feel interested in rather different pursuits.

But even if the Olympic Games came along only once every four years, there were plenty of world-famous, headline-making events all year and every year in between – and my own versatility was unfailingly matched by our back garden's adaptability. It would be Dalymount Park one Sunday and then the following Saturday it would be Wembley Stadium; and there was an uncanny resemblance between the perspiring figure who ran up the couple of glasshouse steps to receive the Football Association of Ireland Cup from the hands of the Taoiseach one week and next week ran up the same steps to receive the English Cup from the King of England himself.

At three o'clock on another Sunday it would be Croke Park and next morning it would be amazingly transformed into Wimbledon. Another time it would be Twickenham and I'd be diving over the line for a last-minute try that brought Ireland the Triple Crown and dashed the English hopes, and on numerous other occasions it was Lords or Sydney and I was the whole English team trying to vanquish the mighty Australian cricketers and the legendary Don Bradman.

The curious thing is that deep down in my heart I know I'm still as invincible an athlete now as I was then – if only I could muster the necessary energy to rise up out of my armchair and turn the little knob on the TV from on to off. Of course there is also a small matter of a few extra stones and more than a few extra years.

Anything else stopping me? Yes, the fact that I'm now a grown-up, mature, wise man-of-the-world, or if I'm not, I must pretend to myself to be. And the world of which I am man is a routine-ridden, pressure-packed, cost-conscious, time-twisted patch, infinitely more demanding than the far-flung playing fields of my youth. Of course there are still challenges to be met and prizes to be won – but moving from boyhood to manhood is like transferring from the marvellous, easy warmth of the amateur ranks to the cold, harsh facts of professionalism.

It's all very, very different from that glorious, shimmering summer in 1936 when the Olympic Games were held in Cork and when, with the greatest ease in the world, I won all the Golds.

My First Death

It was almost too much of a coincidence – J.D. coming in just after a large piece had broken off one of my teeth. He visited us very seldom and I had never once been inside his surgery, yet now here he was, out of the blue, apologising for interrupting our supper while I was running my tongue over the jagged tooth that made me, so unexpectedly, his prospective patient. The suddenness of the catastrophe was such that I would have bared my mouth to him immediately were it not obvious that he had news to tell. He informed us that Mr Kyak had just died.

'Poor soul,' my mother lamented. She made the loss seem personal, though Mr Kyak had been a very solitary and inconspicuous member of our community. Really we knew him only to salute.

'When?' enquired my father.

'About an hour ago.' J.D's mouth twitched in one corner and his parchment-coloured skin was as white as if *he* were the corpse. J.D. was secretary of the Burial Society, a most efficient secretary, a carrier of bad news second to none. His voice dropped, creating a respectful silence. For a moment my tongue paused over my broken tooth while I tried to think of Mr Kyak dead. But death was still unknown to me and remote, as little known and remote as Mr Kyak had been, whereas my broken tooth was a personal horror, abrupt, immediate, foundation-shaking. My tongue probed on.

'The funeral is tomorrow … twelve o'clock,' J.D. announced.

'Twelve o'clock,' my father grunted. 'Have you fixed up the cars?'

'We'll have plenty. Myer and Abram, Jack Caplan, Issy … we won't be short.'

'A cup of tea, Mr Kirsch?' my mother suggested.

'No, thank you.' J.D's parchment cracked into an automatic smile but his mind was elsewhere. Still, the offer was enough to remind him that he hadn't taken his hat off. Like a man brushing flies from his bald pate he swept it off now, revealing his crumpled *yarmulkah,* and darted a look at me. For some reason I guiltily stopped probing at my mouth.

'Who's with him now?' my father asked, bringing my thoughts back to Mr Kyak.

'Cecil.'

'Who else?'

'No one yet. I thought you might go.' J.D. made the suggestion reluctantly. He was always afraid his suggestions would be ridiculed – which they usually were.

'To stay all night? *He* can go.' My father jerked his head in my direction. Once again my tongue was stilled over my tooth.

J.D. wouldn't have minded who stayed with the corpse once Cecil Jacobs had a companion for the night vigil. But I had never watched before – I wasn't even a member of the Burial Society. So J.D. hesitated, pecking in doubt, all the lines on his skin frowning separately.

'He's old enough to start,' my father commented in a dry tone.

'But he's not a member of the Society.'

'I can assure you Mr Kyak won't mind that.'

I gave an involuntary laugh at my father's gallows humour and then immediately regretted it. It made J.D. think I was willing. But I wasn't. I had never seen death before and I had a sudden fear of seeing it now.

'Finish your supper,' J.D. said quickly, 'and then we'll go.'

'I'm finished,' I muttered. How could they expect me to eat supper before going to sit with a corpse?

'You haven't started it yet,' my father pointed out.

'Well, I can't eat any more with my broken tooth.' It was a good excuse for my sudden loss of appetite.

'Let Mr Kirsch see it.'

'Did you break your tooth?' J.D. asked, so unemotionally that I felt slighted.

'*I* didn't break it! It just broke off on its own.'

J.D. stood over me and peered into my mouth. He twisted my head around to the light.

'It's nothing serious,' he said, sitting down again. 'Just rotten in the middle.'

'Rotten?' I echoed in amazement.

'Right through.'

'But I never knew! I haven't had a bad tooth in all my life! It never even pained me!'

'Doesn't have to. I'll fill that easily. Come up to me after the funeral.'

I shook my head, mesmerised at the realisation that I had a tooth rotten right through and never even knew it.

'Well, if you're ready, we'll go,' J.D. suggested.

I got up silently, my tongue chiding at the rotten tooth, my mind appalled as if at some sort of betrayal.

The death house was in a quiet street – a small house made gloomy and foreboding by the half-drawn blinds. J.D. did not knock on the front door but opened it by pulling a string latched inside the letterbox. He led me into the hall, dark and narrow, and up a steep flight of stairs. Almost each step creaked, and the noise made me notice the house's silence.

Reaching the landing, J.D. knocked lightly on one of the doors.

'I think this is the room,' he said.

We heard a quick, heavy tread and the door was flung open by Cecil Jacobs. He was a middle-aged man, a lusty widower, with a stomach of fine protuberance, but his hearty greeting died when he saw me.

'It's all right, we'll elect him at the next meeting,' J.D. assured him testily, anxious as usual to forestall criticism.

'Bugger that,' was the answer.

'He'll be all right,' J.D. repeated. 'There's nothing to it. He's got to start sometime.'

I followed J.D. into the room and shut the door. Immediately I noticed the dry, choking smell. I supposed it to be the smell of death. J.D. and Cecil Jacobs had moved over to the other side of the room where I sensed, rather than saw, a bed on which I sensed, rather than saw, the remains of Mr Kyak.

I sat down on an empty chair, afraid to look, but telling myself that it would be all right to look, that there was nothing to see. So I looked. J.D. and Cecil Jacobs were standing by the side of the bed, their backs to me, gazing down at the corpse of Mr Kyak. Most of his body was hidden by them, but not his head. It was on his head that my gaze fastened. I had taken for granted a sheet hiding everything away, but there was no sheet. Just the bare visage, the colour of paste, looking colder than marble and utterly lifeless. The shock struck me numb and made me forget to breathe.

The phrase 'He fell asleep ...' rushed to mind. I could understand now how tempting such a phrase was. If one did not look, but only said often enough, 'He fell asleep ...' the blow might be softened. Not for me, however, just then. I did not seek a phrase which would make death seem like life; I wanted it made different, set completely apart, so I would not be reminded of it. But, looking on Mr Kyak, he appeared indeed only to have fallen asleep, and I was horrified by the resemblance. I started to tremble, then stopped almost immediately when my ears suddenly began to hear again the voices of J.D. and Cecil Jacobs and I became aware that they were talking about me. I was curious to know what they were saying, but something was preventing me from concentrating on their words and forcing me to keep my gaze on Mr Kyak's dead face. I felt in some deep, obscure way, unwell.

J.D. and Cecil Jacobs turned round. Both of them pinned me with their probing, unhappy looks and J.D. raised his hat for a moment to wipe his forehead. The atmosphere was becoming unbearably heavy. Though the two windows in the room were open at the top, the half-drawn blinds were keeping the smell in and the fresh air out. I loosened my collar.

'Hurry up and get the candles anyway,' Cecil Jacobs was saying.

'I won't be very long,' J.D. replied as he left the room.

Cecil Jacobs continued to stand in the same position, his hat tilted back on his head, his hands clasped behind him so that his belly was urged forward. I could sense his unease.

'Why don't you sit on the other chair?' he suddenly asked me. 'Go on, it's more comfortable.'

'No, not at all, Mr Jacobs,' I gabbled back. 'You sit there. I don't mind the hard chair.'

He continued to look at me for a moment, then shrugged his belly, and reluctantly moved away from the bed. For the first time since I had entered the room, Mr Kyak's body, from the neck down, was revealed to me. It had on only a short cotton pyjama coat that reached hardly as far as the thin buttocks, and even from where I was sitting I could see there was something wrong with the part that was uncovered.

Cecil Jacobs stopped halfway to his chair. 'Take a proper look,' he said. 'Then you can forget it.'

He turned and moved back to the bed. Drawn as if by a magnet, I stood up and joined him beside the corpse. I took a proper look. Mr Kyak's genitals – what had been Mr Kyak's genitals – were now a horrible blue mess, swollen, oozing, and putrid. It was from them that the awful stench was rising. I made no sound at the sight, but a scream shot through me like a rocket, up from my own genitals, up through my frozen body, and out through the hole in my rotten tooth to split into a million sparks in my head. I must have reeled away, for Cecil Jacobs grabbed me by the arm and humped me back to the chair.

'Take it with a laugh, man!' he urged. 'Take it with a laugh! No need to let it get you down.'

I don't remember being actually placed in the chair by him, nor do I remember seeing where he brought the bottle of whiskey from, but the next thing I knew was that a glass was in my hand and he was pushing it to my lips.

'Drink it down! That's the right stuff for this business. Right down with it!' I threw my head back and gulped, too paralysed to be prepared for the kick. It was as if another rocket had been fired off inside me – only this time on the return journey – starting in my head, flashing down through my rotten tooth, and exploding like a burning fountain in my belly.

I gave a long breath and squeezed the tears out of my eyes. The room was a blur, my head was throbbing, and my tooth was giving me hell.

'Feeling better?' Cecil Jacobs asked.

'No. Awful,' I groaned.

'Ah, what's the matter with you? Take these things with a laugh! If that's the worst sight you'll see in your life, you're a lucky man.'

'It's not that,' I replied hastily, not wanting him to know how sick with shock I was.

'What is it then?'

'It's my tooth.'

'Your tooth? What's wrong with it?'

'It broke earlier. It's rotten right through. J.D. is going to fill it tomorrow.'

'Let's see.'

I opened my mouth and Cecil Jacobs pushed his face so close that I could smell the whiskey on his breath.

'Ah yes, I see. Black as the Ace of Spades. Have you bad teeth?'

'No,' I denied. 'I never had a toothache in my life. This happened suddenly. I had no idea it was bad.'

'You probably have a lot more. There's always more than one bad. Is it still paining you?'

'Yes.'

'Here – have some more whiskey. Best thing for a toothache. Don't swallow it quickly – just keep it against the tooth.'

He had it poured out before I could stop him so I put the glass to my lips and allowed a little of the drink to drain against the tooth. I sat there, my jaw bulging slightly, my head ringing, and looked again at Mr Kyak.

'What did he die of?' I asked, almost gargling the whiskey in my cheek.

'You saw for yourself,' Cecil Jacobs replied, putting the bottle to his lips. Seeing him swallow, I involuntarily swallowed also. This time the effect was more pleasurable, so I took another mouthful of whiskey and held it against my tooth.

Cecil Jacobs' answer hadn't told me anything, and the fascination of Mr Kyak's rancid genitals urged me on.

'But how did it happen? What caused it?'

'Too much of what you fancy,' Cecil Jacobs answered, and his belly bounced with mirth.

The idea of Mr Kyak meeting with such an end was too ludicrous and I began to laugh also. The activity made me swallow my last mouthful of whiskey but Cecil Jacobs quickly poured me some more. My whole face was on fire now, not only my tooth, and the atmosphere in the room was like a plague.

'No, really, what *did* cause such a mess?'

'I dunno. Some disease or other. Some germ, it must be.'

'A germ? But couldn't they cure it?'

'Evidently not. I suppose no one knows it's there until it's too late and the rotting has started.'

'And it killed him in the end,' I said, drinking the whiskey now without bothering to rest it against my tooth.

'So it seems,' Cecil Jacobs agreed. 'He's dead, anyway.'

He laughed as if he had made a joke.

'It gets us all in the long run,' he said, 'one way or another. But there's no use worrying about it. You've got to take it with a laugh.'

I could hear Cecil Jacobs' voice fill the room but I wasn't really listening to it. I sat drinking the whiskey and gazing at Mr Kyak's genitals.

'It got him in the end,' I mused. Cecil Jacobs poured me some more whiskey. 'It got him in the beginning,' I half-shouted suddenly. 'Once it started, he was gone. Once the germ started, he was rotting from that moment.'

'So what? Worrying about it won't help. When your number's up, lad, there's nothing you can do.'

Cecil Jacobs drank down his whiskey and poured himself some more. My tongue began to probe again at my rotten tooth, my face felt like a hot balloon, and the horrible smell in the room made me imagine that I was beginning to rise up and float. I looked at Mr Kyak and thought of the germ he had known nothing about until it had been too late. He had been rotting away all the time ...

I jumped up so suddenly that the remains of my drink splashed onto the floor.

'I think I'm going to be sick.'

'What's wrong? What is it?' Cecil Jacobs started to his feet and caught my arm. 'Is it your tooth?'

'No,' was all I could say before I felt too dizzy to continue standing. I plonked back in the chair and held my head in my hands.

'Go on, be sick. Best thing,' Cecil Jacobs urged. 'I'll find the lavatory for you.'

'No,' I groaned, too bad to move. I sat for a while until the dizziness passed and I felt a little better.

Just then J.D. returned, carrying some large candles. He had brought Jack Caplan with him.

J.D. took a look at me and said to Cecil Jacobs, 'What happened to him?'

'How do I know?' Cecil Jacobs barked back. 'You said he'd be all right.'

'His father told me to take him,' J.D. protested. 'It's not my fault.'

Jack Caplan lifted me by the arm.

'I'll take him home.'

'Best thing,' Cecil Jacobs grunted. 'But you'll come back?'

'Yes. I'll be back in ten minutes.'

I allowed Jack Caplan to guide me down the stairs, making a lot of noise as he prevented me from falling.

'Ssh,' he whispered.

'Yes,' I agreed. 'Ssh. Mr Kyak'sh dead.'

He opened the front door and led me to his car. I stood waiting for him to get out his keys. The air seemed to be made of light, strong breezes that lifted me off the ground and tickled my nose. I giggled at Jack Caplan searching for his keys.

'What's wrong with you?' he said.

I laughed back at him, loudly this time.

'Shut up, you fool, and get in,' he hissed.

I thought it was a good joke, Jack Caplan being angry with me, and I got into the car, laughing even more.

'How much whiskey did you have up there?' he asked as he drove off. 'I think you're drunk.'

That was even funnier still and I began to laugh my head off.

'Tell me the joke,' he said.

I couldn't tell him I was laughing at what he said, so I told him something else.

'I broke my tooth. Want to see it?'

I pushed my face up to his.

'Not now, you fool,' he barked. 'I'm trying to drive.'

I was still laughing and at the same time trying to probe my rotten tooth with my tongue. I couldn't do both together, and the more I tried, the more I laughed.

Jack Caplan was glad when he got me home.

'Shall I go in with you?'

'No,' I said, beginning to float away from him. 'Mr Kyak'sh waiting for you.'

He was laughing himself as he drove off.

I wandered up the stairs and into my room. My bed slid up to meet me and I fell onto it. Pulling myself up, I took off my clothes, but when I tried to put on my pyjamas I found myself still fully dressed. Carefully, laughing quietly, I undressed again until I stood naked. Then I put on my pyjama coat and searched for the trousers. Wherever I had dropped them, I couldn't find them now. The more I searched, the more I couldn't find them. It was ridiculous. I lay on the bed in only the pyjama coat, and then I remembered. Of course, poor Mr Kyak had no pyjama trousers so he must have borrowed mine.

I fell asleep wondering how long it might be before I'd get them back. Perhaps not until the Day of Judgement, when the Messiah would send Leviathan throughout all the seven seas to collect the bodies and souls of the Jews for their journey to Paradise. Mr Kyak would be sitting on its snout, my pyjamas decently covering his now-restored genitals, and I would join him, my full set of healthy teeth answering his happy grin. It was the most vivid dream I had ever had, and as the fabulous fish carried us nearer and nearer to God, I was crying with joy.

When I woke in the morning my pillow was wet with tears. But the joy in my heart did not last. It was quickly transformed by an unutterable sorrow when I remembered that this was the day Mr Kyak was going to be put under the ground and I was going to have my rotten tooth filled. 'Take it with a laugh,' Cecil Jacobs had counselled! The only thing I could find to laugh at was the idea that sometime, many millennia in the future, there would come a day when Mr Kyak and I, made whole again, would sail through the gates of Heaven on the back of a huge friendly whale.

The Editor Says ...?

Whh

When I woke up in the morning, Aaron's 'Oh, if only ...' was still in my mind, but at such an early hour of the day I had plenty to do to tackle my own daily agenda. I showered, shaved, dressed, made my breakfast, read the paper, listened to the news on the radio, collected my post, put aside the one or two I'd need to attend to. Then I sat down at my desk and took up my pen to make a few notes on what to reply to the letters, but – and hadn't I warned myself about this before? – some characters you give birth to quickly become like insistent children. Just as I had my pen poised to go to work, my nonagenarian child, Aaron, already had his own pen enthusiastically busy making a list of stories he'd tell Catherine O'Driscoll about Cork's Jews.

I didn't know whether to laugh or cry. I didn't laugh, although it's always welcome to come upon someone enjoying himself, but when Aaron's joy was built on what was no more than optimism, I remembered that his hopes were my baby. Isn't that what I had said to him when he woke me up in the middle of the night: 'OK old man, it's all up to me, isn't it?' That was then but this was now, and when I looked at my watch and saw it was only just gone ten, I decided I still had a bit of time to get rid of my letters as quickly as possible, then think about Aaron's fate.

Well, that man must be telepathic, for before I could write even one word, his telephone rang.

'Catherine?' he said, over-excited.

'Yes, Mr Cohen, this is me. May I drop over to you if you're not busy?'

'I'm never busy, girl. What have I got to be busy with?'

'I'll be there in ten minutes,' and she put the phone down.

Aaron just stood immobile for a while, then replaced his phone and sank back into his chair.

How had her voice sounded? Why had she said so little? Why had she phoned so early in the morning? Perhaps she had bad news for him and wanted to get it off her mind as soon as she could. But if it was that, couldn't she have just told him on the phone? No, no, Aaron thought, if her editor had rejected his suggestion, Catherine was too sympathetic and understanding a person not to duck bringing such an answer herself. But on the other hand, if the answer had been favourable, surely she could have said so on the phone and not kept him a second longer than necessary.

Aaron was all at sea, his thoughts in turmoil. Normally ten minutes was neither here nor there, but not to Aaron, not at this moment. When you're alone and an old man nearly ninety, ten minutes can be torture. He took out his handkerchief and blew his nose. Then he took out a freshly folded clean handkerchief he always carried in another pocket and dabbed his eyes. Noticing on the table the list of places to visit he had been preparing for Catherine, he grabbed at it, about to tear it up. But quickly he changed his mind. He'd have to write the whole list out again if Catherine's news turned out to be good after all. And anyway, if it didn't, it wouldn't be her fault. It would be the fault of her *dumbkopf* editor. 'Humph!' he snorted to himself, remembering the Yiddish curse, 'A fire should burn in his head'. After a slight pause he added, 'God forbid', the cancellation a good Jew was always commanded to add to a curse. It helped him to smile at himself because at his age he couldn't expect to get Heaven to smile on him.

The doorbell rang just then and he quickly wiped the smile off his face. He didn't want to appear confident if, as he feared, there'd be nothing to look confident about.

'Good morning, Mr Cohen. Hope you're keeping well.'

'As before, Catherine, as before. Come in. It's still cold. I presume.' He hoped he would pass for his normal self with no particular worry of special expectation as he ushered her in. 'Please sit down, my girl, take your seat.'

'I was just about to,' she answered.

'Now, before you say anything, I want you to remember that I'm an old man who has had plenty of ups and downs in his life. So you don't have to worry if the news is bad.'

Catherine made him no answer, nor did she smile.

When she remained silent, he had to ask her, 'Did you tell your editor about my idea?'

'I did, Mr Cohen.'

But no other follow-up word from her, good or bad. Why was she playing so *shtum*, Aaron wondered. It must be that she was finding it hard to tell him. Or perhaps her editor hadn't decided yet.

Aaron wasn't going to play around. He'd make her get to the point.

'So what did he say? Yes or No.'

'He said yes,' she answered, releasing her warm, cheeky smile. 'Congratulations, Mr Cohen.'

Aaron nodded his head up and down, up and down with delight and then from side to side as if he hadn't dared to be expecting such good luck. He grasped her hands in his and shook them. 'Congratulations to you too, Catherine. I bet it was you swung it with a brilliant sales talk.'

'No, Mr Cohen, it was you. I just told him what you told me.'

'Now, we must celebrate. I know it's probably much too early for your morning coffee, but I can offer you a glass of wine.'

'No thank you, Mr Cohen, I'm driving.'

'Sensible girl, sensible girl,' and then, after a slight pause, added, 'I would like you to do something for me.'

'Certainly, if I can,' she replied.

'I want you to drop the "Mr" and just call me Aaron. First names are all the fashion these days. I don't doubt that if I met even a baby, it would call me Aaron. You'll do that for me?'

'I'd be very happy to – Aaron,' Catherine answered. 'It's a nice name and you're a very nice person. I've been given a whole week for you to give me all the material I need for the articles, and I'm sure we'll get on together.'

'I have no doubt we will. Now, when do we start on our travels?'

'Right now,' she said, getting up from her chair. 'That's, of course, if you happen to be free.'

'You're certainly a real live wire, not that that surprises me. I'll get my coat.' Aaron was full of almost youthful energy and enthusiasm.

'But where are we going first?' Catherine asked. 'Is it far?'

'Not at all. South Terrace, you know where it is?'

'Yes. I've driven through it, but that's all. What's there for my first lesson?'

Aaron laughed. 'We're going to *shul. Shul* is the Yiddish word for synagogue. I think it's the correct and ideal place to start. So let's go, Catherine, let's go. I'm so looking forward to our week together.'

In the car he explained that they wouldn't be able to enter the synagogue because it was locked, had been for quite a few years.

'But someone must have the keys, mustn't they?' she asked.

'Oh yes, some solicitor has them in his care. The last secretary of the synagogue made some legal arrangement with him to see that the place was kept in good condition, and as soon as the last of us died – which will turn out to be yours faithfully – he was to sell the synagogue and give the money to charity, after paying all expenses of course.'

'But how will he know when – you know what I mean, Aaron.'

'Oh that's all been arranged. I give him a phone call the day I pop off.'

He waited for her laughter, but she didn't laugh.

'Aaron, stop that nonsense about popping off. We all die some time, but you seem as healthy as I am. I can see you reaching a hundred. I certainly intend to visit you on that day, no matter where I'm living.'

'My dear Catherine, waiting for that will keep me going. Now South Terrace is just ahead, so keep on this side of the road. You'll quickly see the synagogue, a blue-painted building, and the locked gates in front of it.'

'Yes, I see it,' she said as she pulled up. 'My goodness, whose idea was it to use that almost garish blue. Not exactly the most suitable colour for a place of worship, is it?'

'No, I suppose it isn't,' Aaron admitted. 'A bit circusy, seasidey I suppose. But in fact blue and white are the colours of the Israeli flag.'

'Yes, of course, I had forgotten that,' she said as they both got out of the car. 'And what's that symbol on the wall above the doors? I've often seen it, but it never occurred to me what it represents. Some holy emblem?'

'No, not that. It's known as *Magen Dovid*, Hebrew for 'Shield of David', said to be the shape of King David's shield. Two interlocking triangles, one pointing up, the other pointing down. They are said to represent God pointing downwards and Man responding upwards. I suppose it's the best-known Jewish symbol, but in fact it didn't become popular until late in the nineteenth century when it began to be used on synagogues. I think it was the Zionist movement that made it so popular. And of course the Nazis made all Jews wear it as a badge on their clothes.'

'Yes, I've seen many pictures of that. Horrible!' Catherine shivered with the recollection.

'Yes, it *was* horrible. But in effect the Nazis made the badge become a symbol of pride to the Jewish people.'

'I must photograph this, and the whole front of the building,' Catherine told him as she took her camera from her bag and snapped the scene from a number of angles.

'My goodness, you're certainly on the ball. I never thought you'd bring a camera.'

'You'll get one of each picture I take this week, Aaron. It's all part of the exchange.'

Having put away her camera she asked, 'What does the synagogue look like inside?'

'Well, it's longer inside than you might think with rows of wide bench-seats down the centre and a row of narrower seats on each side. Halfway down is the *bimah*, an elevated platform with a few steps at each side too. The Cantor, usually known as the *Chazan*, leads the prayers, and at the end of the hall is a built-in cupboard covered by a curtain. Inside it are the Scrolls of the Torah, parchment scrolls that contain all the laws of the Jewish religion. And you can take it from me that there are so many laws and stories in them that it takes a whole year for the Cantor to read one whole section from them each Sabbath before he gets to the end.'

'And what about the women? Do they sit with the men?'

'Yes in Reform synagogues, but not in the Orthodox ones. So ours has a gallery around three sides so that the women can look down on the men but the men would have to look up to see the women. The idea, of course, is to prevent them from looking up and being distracted in their worship. Needless to say, it doesn't always stop them taking a look.'

'Good for them too!' Catherine laughed.

'Hold on,' Aaron responded. 'Do you mean they're entitled to see the women instead of having to pray all the time, or they'll get a crick in their neck if they keep looking up?'

'Oh you're a real smart one, aren't you. Anything else about the synagogue that I need to know? That was a really interesting first lesson.'

'Glad to hear it. And I do have one unusual bit of information for you, but not about the synagogue. Follow me, just a few yards down the road where the river Lee flows. You won't need your camera for this. It's only water.'

She followed Aaron to the protective chain barrier preventing them from getting nearer than a few yards from the river.

'What am I supposed to see in the water?' she asked.

'Sins. You won't actually see them, but it's where they are, or used to be.'

'Sins? What in the world do you mean?'

'I mean *tashlikh*. It's a ceremony observed by some Orthodox Jews on *Rosh-Ha-Shonah*, the Jewish New Year, when they go to a river or the sea to cast their sins into the water while reciting special verses. Sometimes they would also shake the clothes they're wearing so as to clean from themselves every possible sin.'

'Good gracious! Did *you* do that?'

'Not on your life. In fact, just once, when I was young, I saw an old, almost ancient Jew do it. I've never forgotten it. His name was a Mr Jackson. I don't know his first name. There were quite a number of Jacksons in Cork then.'

'Well, well, well! A lovely bit of information. *Tashlikh*. Thank you, Aaron. There can't be many people anywhere who know about that.'

'Not many Jews either. You can bet on that. Now, let's go back to the car and we'll go into town and have lunch together. That suit you?'

'No, I'm sorry, not today. I still have some work in the office from last week that I have to finish off, and then I'll write out as much as I can remember of what you told me. I'll get you to check it for me tomorrow, and I'll bring along my notebook every day. By the way, where are we going tomorrow?'

'Tomorrow I'll take you to Jewtown.'

'Jewtown? Where on earth is that?'

'It's right in Cork city where it used to be. Wait until you see it.'

'Great. Tomorrow then, ten o'clock. Come on, I'll drive you home.'

When that was finished, I put it aside, sat back, and thought. About Aaron and Catherine. In a way I was pleased with them. The happy feeling came from both of them. I thought they were working out just as I had wanted them to. So I should be satisfied with that much. But on the other hand I wasn't quite sure, and I asked myself why. Was there something wrong about Aaron? No, definitely not. About Catherine? Not about her either, though I didn't know her as well as I knew Aaron. Neither of them was even in my mind at that moment. It was myself was in my mind. That was my trouble, my worry about the way I was writing the history of the Cork Jews. While writing it – though I hadn't got very far into it yet – I was subconsciously thinking that I should be giving it more of a novelist's approach: descriptions of people, their looks, shapes, voices, Aaron's home, its location, the Cork streets, Catherine's clothes, etc., etc. When the two characters were together, all I was writing was conversation. But wasn't that what I was supposed to write, Aaron telling Catherine how the Jews came to Cork, lived as Jews, and eventually disappeared? It wasn't supposed to be an academic history. And I wasn't supposed to jump the gun on a proper novel – I wasn't holding a novelist's gun-pen. What I was supposed to be writing was a talkabout, walkabout briefish biography of Cork's Jews. Gotcha! Phew, what a relief to feel I was on the right track after all. So no need to worry – as long as I could forget about Aaron and Catherine for the moment and get on to another chapter of that second volume of autobiography that had started me off on the whole venture in the first place.

Red Letter Days

Coincidence always provides some measure of surprise, but not usually one of very high voltage. However, its first cousin, serendipity, is quite another matter because it detonates not only surprise, but also a captivating emotional shock. Consequently, a combination of coincidence and serendipity can join up in a rare example of a Proustian involuntary memory that is brought back to life accompanied by its material witness. On 2 October 2002, I experienced such an occurrence.

On the morning of that day, I read a review of a book based by the writer on a cache of secret letters that had passed between his parents before they married, and on discovering it in his widowed mother's house before she died, he 'purloined' it and used it as the material of his book.

After reading the review, I later that day accidentally upended a pile of old, long-forgotten manuscript jotters from the back of a dusty shelf and out of them fell a cache of letters. I had no idea what they could be, but to my amazement I found they were letters that had been written by me in 1968 from my Dublin flat where I was living after returning from my thirteen-year sojourn in London and to my further astonishment they had been addressed to my parents, to whom it had been my practice to send news of my doings every week. The serendipitous discovery of these thirty-four year old letters must have been kept by my mother because of the nature of their contents, cherished by both her and my father. I concluded that after my father died she had sent the letters back to me to ensure that not only would they survive her own death, but that as long as I lived, the letters would always be in my care to keep their pride in me alive. Reading the letters, I could easily see in my mind's eye the image of my parents re-reading them again and again. More than that, however, those so long-forgotten weekly reports revived in my memory, as if in a moving film, the two most important events that enabled my speculative return from England to Ireland to set down permanent roots in my own country.

The events were my founding of the 'New Irish Writing' page in the *Irish Press*, and the production in the Gate Theatre of my translation from the Irish of *The Midnight Court*, adapted for the stage by Sean McCann and myself. Somewhat uncanny too was the near-enough coincidence of their dates: the first 'New Irish Writing' page appeared in print on 20 April 1968, and the first performance of *The Midnight Court* took place on 3 June of the same year. The contents of my letters gave my parents a glimpse of what the birth of the first page of 'New Irish Writing' entailed, and particularly more than just a glimpse of the traumas and crises preceding *The Midnight Court*'s rise of the curtain which the ordinary theatre-goer could never have imagined. My belated discovery of the letters returned by my mother has enabled me to re-experience those exciting days.

February 1968
Dear Folks,
The Midnight Court: *I had a phone call from Sean McCann on Thursday to say that he had a call from Phyllis Ryan, (Director of Gemini Productions), who said that Barry Cassin thought the play was great and should go like a bomb but that he was booked up all the summer and could not free himself. Phyllis had consequently phoned Michael Bogdanov, who was interested in the possibility of directing the play, and she was to see him yesterday to give him the script. She said she wanted two more copies of the script – which fortunately I had – and a copy of my published*

translation by next morning. As I did not trust the post, I went down to her home in Rathmines to drop them in to her. She was there herself and we had a grand chat. She is a very neat, spruce and attractive person, I'd say in her late thirties. She was full of enthusiasm and revealed more of her plans. She had decided not to use the Eblana but has booked the Gate from June onwards and hopes it will run throughout the tourist season! She already has her backer for it – she said he is an American and it was for him she wanted a copy of my translation. If Bogdanov did not happen to want to direct, she had others in mind. And she was due to meet the directors of the Gate to put before them her summer programme which, she said, is our play. So production does seem nearer. I liked her and am sure I shall get on well with her – she is also keen to see the full-length play I am working on, though as yet it is only in the drafting stage.

'New Irish Writing': I started to write to authors on Wednesday and today had the first reply – a terribly friendly and encouraging letter from Brian Friel. But he hasn't written any stories for two years and unless his agents have one that hasn't appeared in Britain, I shall probably have to do without him. But his letter couldn't have been warmer. Liam Miller of Dolmen Press was delighted with the news about the play and about 'New Irish Writing' and is being extremely helpful in showing me unpublished work by the various Irish poets which are on his list for future production. He also said to me that Maurice Fridberg, the publisher of The Hourglass Library, *told him that he is bringing out a book of my stories! This astounded me but I wouldn't pay too much attention to it. Fridberg obviously said that between the Sunday I saw him and the Friday when he went away but whether he had yet read the five stories I sent him on Monday and was basing his comment on that, I don't know.*

    Love, David

April 26th, 1968
Dear Folks,
Glad you liked the first page of 'New Irish Writing'. Reactions here have been without exception favourable and I feel it will quickly establish

itself as something people will look forward to every Saturday.

I have nothing of particular interest to report. We did not see Mike Bogdanov this week as Telefís sent him away on some job but from next week we shall be down to the beginnings of the real slogging. I have finished the re-writing – the first re-writing, that is – because after Bogdanov reads it closely we shall do further re-writing! I am also seeing on Saturday the chap who is doing the music and Phyllis Ryan has already started assembling the cast. A few she wants are not certain yet as they won't commit themselves until they see a script and read the part being offered to them. Today I am lunching at Trinity with Brendan Kennelly, whose poetry I published last week. He is a lecturer in English in Trinity (early thirties) and reckoned to be among the leading Irish younger poets. I have not yet met him but when he sent me his poems (I have two more from him for later) I thought they could be improved. I asked his permission to make suggestions, and when he gave me the go-ahead I sent him a long letter of alterations and reasons. To my surprise and delight he welcomed almost all of them – indeed made further improvements himself – and was very grateful. He also – I am told – has made no secret of the fact that he made changes at my suggestion – not all poets would want that kind of thing known so he must be a nice chap. From Kerry. After lunch I'll spend the rest of the day in the Press getting No.2 fixed up. I'll hold this letter till to-morrow to send you the page, and will, of course, send you each week's page.

Love, David

May 4th, 1968
Dear Folks,
Herewith today's page which I think you'll find amusing. As you'll see the story took up more space than intended and had to have a runover onto another page. This is a bit worrying as I have a few stories coming up that are even longer but I suppose I'll just have to drop the poetry now and again to accomodate them. There are still a lot of headaches getting this page out, especially on the Friday, but I think things should smooth out soon. Certainly the Irish Press must be very pleased with

the reception. Although not one person has, so far as I know, written in to the Editor about the page – and this amazes me – the verbal reports keep coming in. And today comes the first reaction of the Irish Times – an announcement of a £100 short story competition for new writers. Frankly, I am very pleased at this – they are only doing my work for me in stimulating the new writers. Only one can win the award and all the good stories that fail to win must inevitably come to me! The competition closes on August 1st but I am not worried about getting no good stories from new writers until then because I have three months' stories by established writers lined up! And anyway I may have at least one new story writer in the bag myself and definitely have a few new poets. I am thinking of doing an editorial welcoming the Times' announcement but I don't think I'd be allowed as it might seem too cheeky.

Hardly any news this week about The Midnight Court – I'm glad to say. One of the actors who had been offered a part asked to read the script first. Having read it he phoned Phyllis to say it was the dirtiest play he had ever read! Naturally he took the part. It isn't dirty, just very, very bawdy. No doubt things will start to move this week as rehearsals start on the 20th.

Incidentally – remember the little book of Six Poems by me that the Dolmen Press did in a limited edition years ago? An uncut copy was sold last week at a book auction for £13. Of course the reason is that early Dolmen Press productions on their hand-press are now collectors' items.

Needless to say I picked Sir Ivor for the Guineas, to continue my run of big race successes! I didn't see the 1,000 Guineas so had no selection for it.

Re the Ernest Gebler play – I had seen this in London when it was first put on and watched it again. Very good. Gebler used be accepted as an Irish writer, as he lived so long in Dublin and was first married to Edna O'Brien before she started her novels; and I had a story by him in Irish Writing. Don't forget my story next Friday at 11 on BBC Light Programme, Radio 2.

We're just having a thunderstorm here.

Love, David

May 11th, 1968
Dear Folks,
Sorry I just can't write a proper letter this week as I'm up to my eyes with Midnight Court *work – piles of more re-writes and new songs to be done. Going to Maureen Toal's house on Monday night to meet the cast and hear the music. I've already heard it actually and it's good.*

    Thought the story on the BBC reasonably well read.

    Love, David

May 18th, 1968
Dear Folks,
Again this will be a scrap of a letter. I thought it was impossible for things to get more rushed but I was wrong. Being involved in a show of this nature is an astounding experience. The meeting at Maureen Toal's house was not a great success because only two of the cast had ever seen a script and the copies had not come from the typists. So the cast were reading odd pages from the only copy available and so of course were getting all the wrong impressions. To add to the trouble, the chap doing the music couldn't come, so he taped the music and sent the tape which didn't work so he was phoned and arrived at 11.30 and his performance of the music at that hour after a day's work left a great deal to be desired. Consequently there is a state of chaos at the moment but another meeting at Toal's will take place on Sunday when things should be fixed up. But much re-writing will take place well into next week. I am now entering the period when I am scared stiff that the audiences will find the show offensive and be disgusted with it. Martin Dempsey, who was offered one of the two male leading parts, read a script a few days ago and turned it down flat on the grounds that the whole thing was in bad taste. This is a very valid view and is in no way prejudiced. In fact he said that he has read all four translations of the poem and thinks mine the best. But I fear many others may take the same view of the show. However, we are mounting a terrific publicity barrage starting in the Sunday papers this weekend, so we shall see.

    I liked Maureen Toal – a very straightforward and considerate per-

son. I also was mad about Eamonn Keane, John B. Keane's brother.
He is a quiet chap who is a wonderful talker when anyone talks to him.
He kept going around telling people that the first two pages of my
translation should be in every general and schools' anthology of English
poetry! But I fell for him even before he started saying this! And he was
dead sober – he can't drink as he would be a sponge if he went back on
it! The others were OK but some of them were acting all the time. We
still have to fill the part Martin Dempsey turned down and are after
someone even better – Eamonn Kelly – but the chances of getting him
are not too bright. He has done a lot of British comedy TV work –
mainly as an Irish tramp.

Late news: The Kelly we're looking for – I've just heard – is
David, not Eamonn. Better still but we'll never get him. You've seen
him often on TV – lately in the Hugh Leonard play about the men and
women on the Retreat. I'm rushing off to a 10 a.m. meeting. What a
wonderful letter from MacLiammoir – full of praise for the page –
suggesting we meet!!!

Love, David

May 27th, 1968
Dear Folks,
A quick interim report to let you know how things are going. And to be
Irish I must say I don't know how things are going. Absolute chaos seems
to reign ... but, by God, what an experience it is! I am still feverishly re-
writing. Most of the harder re-writes are now done but there are still
pieces left and a very difficult song and bits to be re-done and lines to be
changed round and re-written and God knows what else. And if you
think that's all ... The first official rehearsal started on Monday morning
and was to be devoted to a reading of the script. Well, we started off
minus three of the cast. The new girl, signed on last week mainly to sing
the love-song, had food-poisoning; the other young girl (there are four
females in the cast) just didn't put in an appearance; and the part of the
old man had still not been cast as David Kelly turned it down – partly because of the type of play and partly because he didn't feel the part was in

his line. By the afternoon session, however, the old man had been cast and was there. A very good actor named Arthur O'Sullivan who had been mentioned a month ago for the part but whom the producers and the director had seemed to have some artistic prejudice against. I think he'll be first-class. But that was all? Not bloody likely. We are supposed to have two musicians – who are on stage as part of the crowd all the time. They are a fiddler and an accordionist. We had the fiddler the day before at Maureen Toal's and he was marvellous, but up to that time no accordionist could be found who'd take the job. Consequently, on Monday morning it was decided not to have one at all but use the fiddler only – a decision which pleased me and others who don't like an accordion. BUT came Tuesday and a message from the fiddler that his wife had had a heart attack and he had to give up the job! So as of last night, still no fiddler. Then a very good girl was coming over from London to do the costumes. Needless to say, she phoned yesterday that her mother had been taken to hospital so she was out!!! Quite unbelievable – and I do sympathise with the producers who have to combat such trials. A lot of cutting has been done of too bawdy lines – most of which I agreed to without much worry but some of which I was sorry to lose. But what can one do? Anyway they are rehearsing eight hours a day, in two sessions each day. I have been at two sessions as I've been told to stay home and finish the writing! I can certainly say that I'll never again go into a theatre without an uneasy conscience after seeing what goes into a production. It is quite sensational how the producer and the cast work and slog through things – some scenes he makes them do up to twenty times and their willingness and good humour is astounding. Indeed the early rehearsals are hilarious because they are mostly reading, and worrying only about the actions and movement so the amount of clowning they do and the way they twist the lines is stupendous. Sean and I and Philip O'Brien, the backer, are often stretched out with laughter. It is a kind of company – the company of stage people, I mean – which could easily get into one's blood.

Full cast were present yesterday – thanks be.

Love, David

June 15th, 1968
Dear Folks,

Heat-wave still on here. I've not been in touch with the show so don't know how bad the audiences have been or whether anything has been fixed about Cork.

Herewith the Irish Press *– again I have a splash as you'll find a book review and a review of my radio play. What a headline – the poor bard must be turning in his grave.*

I'm told the Poet Laureate, Day Lewis, is interested in sending me poems for 'New Irish Writing'. As you'll recall, I had him in Irish Writing *and* Poetry Ireland. *I'll write him.*

Love, David

June 22nd, 1968
Dear Folks,

Hope you are keeping well and that the Boss is having a good Ascot. I watched most of it on TV and it seemed that one should have been able to keep out of trouble.

The play is still on and enters its fourth week next week. I don't know at the moment if that will be its last week. We got our cheque for the first week's royalties. Between us we got £36 but from that had to be taken £22.10.0 being half the fee for the composer. We had agreed to this as with musicals the music is usually given to the management with the script whereas in this case the management had to engage a composer and pay him. That left us with £14 between us, and my own half was reduced by £6 to pay for the special tickets I had got. So I ended up with £1!! But I am satisfied. The second week's figures were very bad – the heat-wave did it – lucky if we get half the first week's, but even at that I won't grumble as it will be around £7-£9 for me; but the third week is much improved and should be at least as good as the first. Indeed, if to-night is full (and the weather here is not now all that summery) it should be more than the first.

Love, David

29th June, 1968
Dear Folks,

Not a great deal of news from my end. The play will run one more week so that it will have had five weeks. Business has picked up a bit and the producers are now sorry they didn't take up the chance of doing a sixth week. The £22.10.0 to the composer is the end of our obligation to him (he also got £22.10.0 from the producers). We now have the returns from the 2nd and 3rd weeks. The 2nd week, which was the really bad one, earned Sean and me £10.10.0 each, and the 3rd week about £17.10.0 each. We had hoped for just a little more from the 3rd week. From what we hear, the 4th week will be at least as good as the 3rd. All in all I should get around £70 out of it. We shall not be going to Cork at the moment and it doesn't seem likely later in the year either as it would be a difficult thing to re-assemble all the cast, and to have a new cast means new rehearsals and production costs.

I had a phone call from Seán Ó Faoláin last Sunday to come and meet his daughter, Julia, who is over from America, but I just couldn't go. He'll probably be in touch with me again however, as she'll be here a few weeks

I was delighted to get the Boss's letter about Ascot. What magnificent form he was in. If it was old times we'd have cleaned up. I fancied one or two of the ones he did but doubt I'd have been on the mark as well as he was. I've just been out shopping and saw Liam O'Flaherty (who has a flat near me) shopping too with a copy of The Irish Field (which is the Irish equivalent of The Sporting Chronicle) under his arm so it seems he is a horsey man too. Incidentally, I have tried to get a story from him for the page but there's no response. I'm told he has turned very sour and does no more writing. I'll be watching Sir Ivor slam them to-day of course. Enclosed is to-day's page – I'm not myself mad about the stuff in it but feel the story caters for a section of the population that I mustn't neglect – the many who'll appreciate a sort of folk-tale with a relevance for contemporary official-pill-less Ireland! Next week I'm having four new writers. And C. Day Lewis has promised to send me some poems, which has tremendously bucked the

Press *editor who thinks he is a great scoop (though it's not really – I'm sure he would send poems to any reputable paper who would pay him.) But they've got an exclusive interview with him which they're holding until I have his poems and they'll run the interview the day before. And John B. Keane specially wrote for me a most delightful short story, just a little bit naughty too!*

Love, David

July 13th, 1968
Dear Folks,
Not a great deal to report this week. The royalties for the final week of the show were quite good – we got nearly £22 a man. This means that after paying expenses for tickets and drinks and things like that I had over £65 left, which is quite satisfactory. I have heard no more about the hotels version so imagine that it has come too late to be feasible for this year. The champagne party was a very quiet affair backstage. Maureen Toal made a nice little speech to which I responded.

I am hacking my way through the last act of my TV play but the long delay since I finished the first two Acts has messed it up a great deal and I don't think it's going to be good enough. But I hope to finish it next week and have it out of the way so as I can start something else. The Dolmen Press will be publishing a collection of my poetry next spring! It may only be in paperback form but I shall be pleased to see my poems in a book and also to find out just how tough the Irish reviewers will be. I should very soon also be getting some money from Liam Miller for the sales of The Midnight Court.

Love, David

24th September, 1968
Dear Folks,
A quick note to let you know that at 11 p.m. last night in the Red Bar I was appointed Literary Editor of the Irish Press. *(By a quirk of fate, drinking at another table was Ben Kiely, the last Lit Ed of the Press, now on holidays from the US).*

I did not get the £1,500 I asked for. Instead Tim Pat made me an offer: £1,650!!! For the next few minutes there followed the unique occurrence of me trying to beat him down to what I had asked for. But he stood firm!

Must rush – full details in Saturday's letter.
Love, David

The foregoing letters were the only ones in the cache my mother sent me. No doubt I'll re-read them many times, because every time I do, there will be in my mind the image of my parents re-reading them again.

Lithuania by the Lee

Early morning, Aaron was sitting in his favourite chair, restlessly fidgeting, waiting for Catherine. When he had told her that Jewtown was to be their next day's destination, he had felt a shiver of excitement, a frisson that was virtually a new experience. He would be going home to Cork's Jewtown, where he had been born. He would be going home on almost his ninetieth birthday, more than twenty years since he had last been there. That was when he had moved to the city centre, and soon afterwards the few remaining Jewish residents had emigrated to London or New York or Israel, there being then no one and nothing left for him to see. At first he felt he still belonged to Jewtown and it to him, but as the years accumulated, not even its name was remembered except by him, and Hibernian Buildings, as originally christened, reclaimed its identity. From that time on Aaron accepted that he would be no more than a shade in its old streets.

He rose from his chair, angry with himself for everything. Why had he made such a fool of himself? Why had he persuaded Catherine that he'd help her to write about the story of Cork's Jews? Why in the name of God had he not remembered that Jewtown would have to be in their itinerary? He had known for years and years that the real Jewtown existed now only in his mind, and no matter how much longer he might live, he would never want to go back there and have to gaze on the many changes that must have taken place. So how in the world had he been such an imbecile to behave like an excited child when her editor gave her the go-ahead? He had been a fool, no, not just a fool – an old fool. Yesterday's old fool, for today was today, and all through the night, tossing and turning in his bed, he was praying to the darkness to stun him into a heavy, dreamless sleep. But all he could do was lie there through the hours, trying to think of some way, some scheme, by which he could somehow avoid going to Jewtown. When he got up, however, he knew he had no alternative but to forget what he had long promised to himself, and fulfil what he had now promised to Catherine. He would go with her to Hibernian Buildings, show her what and where had been his Jewtown, a real place that never in over a living century had even been named on the map of Cork. Had it by chance been thus identified, recorded by the cartographer's mark, perhaps that could have helped him to repel all the new sights and still see only his own inner-eye images. And suddenly he realised that it was fate had chosen him to impart to the people of Cork the story of Jewtown, where so long ago his antecedents had, as refugees, found a home in their city.

'I am Cork's last Jew,' he heard himself say aloud. 'I am a *kohen*, a descendent of Aaron, our first priest, and I go there now to bring to Jewtown my last priestly blessing.' He shivered, his embarrassment quickly melting into his pride.

At that moment Catherine's ring sounded at the door.

On the drive to Jewtown Aaron was particularly silent. Catherine wondered if he was unwell or maybe worrying about something. If it was the latter, could it be that visiting Jewtown might somehow be upsetting him? He had seemed perfectly happy about it when he had told her on the previous day that it was where they'd be going next. Had he lived there once? If he had, one could hardly blame him if that was his trouble. After all, he was the last Jew in Cork. With the rest of them gone, he must feel like no more than a living ghost in the city.

'There isn't far to go now,' Aaron murmured. 'We're nearly there.'

'That's good,' Catherine answered, trying to sound encouraging, thinking that despite the heavy traffic, the quicker they got there, the better.

Aaron was indeed unsettled and nervous. Eastville, the street where he was born, would be more than just a trial for him. He feared it would even bring back all the heartache of his long past. Could he face that? He had to.

'Pull up here,' he said immediately they reached the end of Hibernian Buildings, 'and follow me, Catherine.'

He led her past two rows of houses which faced each other across a narrow street named Geraldine Place, then around its end to face another narrow street of about only a dozen equally small houses. Catherine said nothing, waiting for Aaron to offer some explanation of why he had made a bee-line to this particular street out of the many others she had caught a glimpse of when reaching Hibernian Buildings.

'This, Catherine, is Eastville,' Aaron said quietly. 'This is where many of the earliest Jews who came from Lithuania settled, and along with a smaller group who preceded them, they all became the Cork Jewish community. A room in one of the houses had to double as a sort of synagogue for them and they prayed in that room every day. I don't know which house it was, but in 1884 they rented a room in Marlborough Street from the Cork Branch of the National League and they fitted it up as a small synagogue until they were in a position to build a proper one in South Terrace, which you saw yesterday. I was born here, in Eastville, in the house about halfway down. It hardly matters which one it was. They all looked the same inside and out.

'Now Catherine, if I may have the car keys, I'll sit in there for a while while you look around and take all the photographs you want. Take your time, my girl. I have a lot to remember. And a lot to forget.'

'Would you like me to sit with you?'

'No, my dear, no. I'll be perfectly all right. Whenever you're ready, we have the whole morning for me to show you around Jewtown. See you soon.'

Catherine took only two photographs, one of a house front and the other from the street end to provide a long view perspective of the street itself. In any event, all the houses now looked quite modern to her and must surely bear little or no resemblance to themselves of nearly one and a half centuries before. What an old world, no, almost an ancient world it would have been. And when Aaron was growing up, that old world would still have been around him. Yes, more than likely that was what suddenly made him return to the car. Poor Aaron. Catherine had her own bad memories too, but his might well be far worse than hers.

She had left him long enough by himself. It was time for her to go back to him. He might need sympathy. No, he'd hardly look to her for that, a young girl like her. She must be careful not to be too forward or presumptuous. But companionship was always worth something. If he was suffering, at least she could offer him that.

'Are you all right, Aaron, perhaps you'd prefer to go home,' she said as she opened the car door.

'My goodness, no such thing. It was just seeing my birthplace that threw me. I hadn't been back once since I left Jewtown. But when one gets to my age, one has had plenty of time not only to recall the past, but also to learn to live in the present. You know, you need to be as old as me to handle two different worlds every day. Now, here are your keys and let me get out. There's a lot more for you to see, and a lot more for you to hear about and write about. Ready?'

'Right and ready. Where to?'

'Just around the corner, it'll take us just one minute. Monerea Terrace. The place where the very first Jews to arrive in Cork found a home.'

'Cork's first Jews ever! That's really something,' Catherine exclaimed.

'I thought it would give you a starting-point,' Aaron said happily, as if he felt like a tour guide capturing his audience's excited interest.

Monerea Terrace was a wide street that startled Aaron when they entered it.

'Look at that,' he said. 'See that row of houses. Well, when I was still living in Jewtown, just across from all that row of houses was a wall and behind it rose three gasometers, two of them very big and round, like huge drums, and very high. I was always fascinated by their size and strangeness. And now they're gone. I miss them already.'

'Never mind them, Aaron. Tell me, when did these first Jews arrive?'

'It was about in the early 1870s. Maybe between ten and twenty of them, and all of them came from neighbouring villages in Lithuania. They thought they had arrived in America, which was supposed to be their destination. Of course they hadn't a word of English, and when their boat docked, they heard the crew shouting "Cork! Cork!" and understandably they took it to mean "New York! New York!" So they disembarked, found one of the houses looking for tenants, and there they were.'

'Just like that?'

'More or less. Of course, it wasn't easy for them to get from the harbour to an area in the city where they saw the empty house. I got to know them when I was growing up and they often told me their story. By then they could all speak English. The men had been very well educated in their bible, the Old Testament, and in Hebrew, although Yiddish was their spoken language. That sort of upbringing, the quest for knowledge, was second nature to them. They learned English quite quickly, mostly by reading the *Cork Examiner*.'

'I'll tell my editor that,' Catherine said with a laugh. 'That'll tickle him.'

'It will. But better still is their story of the first day they spent in the house. Almost immediately after they went in, a crowd of local men and women from neighbouring houses started to gather outside, shouting and trying to look in through the front window and knocking at the door. Of course the Jews had no idea what these people wanted, but from their own experiences with local pogroms in Lithuania which was governed by Russia, they expected the worst. So they locked the door and window, and prayed. One of their men was their own Rabbi and he led the prayers. After a while the shouting outside suddenly died and someone started knocking again at the window. The Rabbi went over to see who it was. It was a priest, who signalled to the Rabbi to open the door. Which he did, feeling certain that he had nothing to fear from a holy man, and the priest somehow made him understand that the people did not intend to hurt them,'

'But the Jews could hardly have known that, could they?' Catherine protested.

'Well, the priest persuaded the Rabbi to come out, and when he did, all the Jewish men and women joined him. As soon as the priest explained that the neighbours had been calling to them just to see them, because they had never seen a Jew in their lives, they laughed with relief. The priest shook hands with every one of them and told his parishioners to follow suit. The Rabbi thanked the priest and then invited them all into the house. When they saw that the Jews were ordinary mortals – just men and women like themselves with a few children like their own – and seeing that there was no furniture in the room and that they had little possessions, some of the neighbours slipped away and returned within minutes with food, and stools to sit on and even little dolls for the children. A couple of women carried in even an old mattress. And would you believe, one old woman brought a picture of Jesus for them! You know, from that moment on, these Jews, all the way from Lithuania, and these Cork Christians, their first neighbours, were the best of friends for the rest of their days. And best friends of all were the Rabbi and the priest. The priest used visit him every week, and soon, every Sunday evening, if both of them were free, they had an arrangement to get together for an evening of two-handed solo. It turned out that both of them were lovers of the game, and in no time at all they became the friendliest, most enthusiastic rivals.

'What do you think of that, Catherine, what do you think of that?'

'It's a great story, a great human story. You know what, I don't want to sound sort of sentimental, but what you've just told me makes me proud of being born in Cork.'

'Shake on it, my girl,' Aaron said, offering his hand, 'that makes two of us.'

'I'm glad it does, Aaron, very glad ...' She started to say something, but then hesitated.

'What is it? Something on your mind?'

'Nothing really important, and I don't want to spoil our morning by asking you silly things that you may not want to talk about.'

Aaron chuckled and made her link arms with him.

'No, my dear girl, you can ask me anything you like. Something about Eastville, is it, because I left you there so suddenly?'

'Not because you left me to go back to the car. It was that I thought readers would be keen to know what the inside of the house where you were born was like.'

'A very sensible question, and I can give you the answer. I was five when my mother told me how ghastly the place was the day they went in. It was very small. There were just two attic bedrooms and the stairs leading up to them was in the kitchen, and there was a pantry off this. In the front of the house there was one small room next to a very small, narrow hall. There was no covering on the floors and little in the line of furniture more than the barest necessities. All that was bad enough, but there was much worse to come. On the very first night they found that the two attic bedrooms were swarming with bugs.'

'Oh my God,' Catherine exclaimed, shivering with horror.

'And because the only light they had was from candles, they could do nothing about it until daylight, when they stripped the beds and scalded the walls, the floors and the beds with boiling water. Then they dried them and sprinkled them with carbolic powder. My mother said that was all you could get at the time. It took them about a fortnight to repeat the process of scrubbing the floors every day before the whole place was clean and safe.'

'And what did they have to pay for somewhere like that to live in? How much was their rent?'

'I don't remember exactly,' Aaron said, 'it's so long ago. But I'm fairly sure that in old money it was either five shillings or seven-and-six a week. There are other things too I can tell you about Jewtown. So let's go into the city and we'll have lunch some-where nice and I'll tell you some more of the early Cork Jews' history.'

'That would be great,' Catherine said, 'and I know exactly where we'll go. We'll have lunch in your house. I'm sure you have a kitchen, and I'll make the lunch for us. I have a nice parcel of food on the back seat and there's nothing in it that your Jewish dietary laws wouldn't allow you eat – I made sure to check on that first. I've come prepared to insist that we should have lunch together today just by ourselves, and talk and get to know each other. So come on, Aaron, I won't take no for an answer.'

Aaron stood there, speechless for a while.

'Well, any objections?'

'Catherine, I'm an old man and I've never had a charming young woman make lunch for me.'

'And I'm a young woman who has never had the chance to make lunch for a charming old man. So let's be off then.'

'With pleasure, my girl. I'm honoured.'

Father Figures

I was nine at the time, my father about ninety-nine – or so it seemed to me. Not that he had a bushy white, old man's beard, or indeed any sort of beard. But he smoked, which proved to me that he must be old, because in those days you had to be old to smoke. Later on though, when the first scare of the connection between cigarettes and cancer was reported, he gave up smoking for the rest of his life.

I spent as much time as I could with him in his small picture-framing factory. I loved the smell of glue that always hung in the air and the carpet of coloured wood-shavings that were like leaves shed by the forest of tall, shiny mouldings leaning against the walls.

Inside the ramshackle office at the back he would sit at an untidy roll-top desk doing his bills and accounts while I explored the cupboards and drawers all around. The wide, shallow drawers housed hundreds of glossy prints which he framed and sold to shops and dealers all over the city and county. I found magic in them, not because they had come from far-off Switzerland – wondrous though that was – but because of the exotic subjects and rich, throbbing hues. Some of them were what my father called 'scenes' – sheep grazing serenely, swans riding their mirror-image on a placid river, the farmyard's seasons, mountains against a dramatic sky – but the ones that I returned to again and again were the 'holy pictures'. Their names added to their mysterious spell – the Infant of Prague, The Agony in the Garden, Perpetual Succour, Virgin and Child, and the most intriguing one of all, Sacred Heart. It depicted a handsome, sharp-featured man, bearded, his head, shoulders and chest filling the large canvas, his face looking down and slightly sideways with an expression that, if it wasn't actually absent-minded, appeared to betray no great concern. I wondered at his seeming indifference to his terrible injuries – not only was his brow blood-spattered from the band of thorns that encircled his head, but there was a big hole in his chest to expose a swollen, lurid heart.

I knew who he was of course, for I had seen another picture of him hanging in every classroom at school. In that one he was nailed to a cross and wore only a large handkerchief around his willy. His face was sunk on his chest, as if he was asleep, and sometimes, when the sun came through the classroom window and spotlit him clinging to the wall, if I peered at him through half-closed eyes I could imagine that he was really stretched out on a golden strand, drying after a dip and happily sun-bathing.

'That's Jesus Christ, Daddy,' I told my father. He was always telling *me* things so I was glad whenever I had a chance to show him that I knew a thing or two myself.

'Yes,' he replied, preoccupied at his desk. 'If you say so.'

'Who *was* Jesus Christ, Daddy?'

At this my father stopped writing and gazed into space. He closed one eye for a moment and allowed a ball of cigarette smoke to roll out of his mouth.

'He was someone who tried to be all things to all men. Not a completely unusual aspiration for a Jew. We had a few like that before him and we've had a few since.'

My father's reply to my questions were frequently puzzling but this one completely baffled me. I had never known him to be wrong before, yet surely what he was saying now couldn't be correct.

'But Christ was a Catholic. Daddy,' I argued, adding shakily, 'wasn't he?'

He lit another cigarette and blew the smoke out over my head. I sniffed it gratefully and waited for elucidation.

'An understandable confusion, son, under the circumstances. Incorrect, nevertheless. Jesus Christ was born a Jew and died a Jew. He has even been hailed as "King of the Jews".'

'But Catholics pray to him, don't they? And they believe he was the son of God.'

'So he was, my boy, so he was.'

I sighed. Here was yet another conundrum-answer, but fortunately my sigh made my father relent and amplify.

'We're all sons of God, my boy.'

'Is God a Jew then?' I asked. I had never thought of God as being anything.

My father smiled widely with anticipation and took a huge pull on his cigarette.

'Of course God is a Jew. Do you think I'd have anything to do with a non-Jewish God?'

By now I was beginning to feel just a little bit mad with my father. When he was in his jokey mood it was almost impossible to get a straight answer out of him.

'But if Christ was born a Jew and died a Jew, when was he a Catholic?' I was determined to keep him to the point.

'Never! He was a Jewish teacher who went around preaching the word of God, with a few little twists of his own.'

My father stubbed out his cigarette, emptying his mouth and nose simultaneously of the last puff of smoke. Then he continued.

'A lot of people took exception to his influence and so they killed him. Of course killing a man for his ideas gets rid of the man, but it never gets rid of his ideas. That's something the human race hasn't even yet learned. Anyway, some time after his death, *after* his death, mind you, a band of his followers adapted his teachings and made a new religion out of them. They called it Christianity – Christianity: Christ. Satisfied?'

I nodded.

Of course I wasn't satisfied, not quite. At the back of my mind another, much larger problem was forming. If Christ had been a Jew, then strictly speaking all the Christians who came after him were really Jews too from way back. The fact that they may have called themselves something else was immaterial. The revelation made me dizzy with shock.

Slowly I closed the drawer on the picture of Christ's suffering Jewish heart and idly opened the one next to it. Staring up at me was another print I had seen hanging up on the school wall – St Patrick banishing the snakes from Ireland. A big man, perched on a rock, wearing a curiously shaped hat and holding a long, curiously shaped stick. He stared into the distance while hundreds of snakes slithered down from the rock and into the sea. I wondered how he had persuaded them to leave. The Pied Piper of Hamelin had got rid of the rats – and of the children too – by playing a tin whistle, but there was no suggestion that St Patrick played any instrument. Yet he might well have, in exactly the same way as the Hamelin man. I had a book at home with a picture of an Indian sitting on the ground playing a tin whistle and in front of him a snake was weaving from side to side, captivated by his tune. Perhaps whoever wrote my Irish history book thought that to get rid of the snakes by playing a tin whistle wasn't quite a dignified way for St Patrick to do it and so it wasn't mentioned. And of course what was important was not the business with the snakes but the fact that St Patrick had brought Christianity to Ireland.

Suddenly it struck me that if the Irish hadn't been Christians before St Patrick arrived, then they must, like Jesus, have been Jews. Come to that, St Patrick had really been a Jew too, originally!

This was an even more shattering discovery than that Jesus himself had been a Jew. I couldn't credit it without some authoritative confirmation.

'Daddy, before Saint Patrick came to Ireland, were the Irish all Jews?'

'Most unlikely.'

'What were they?'

'I presume they were pagans. You see, before Christianity started, not everybody was Jewish. Those who weren't Jews were pagans. That is, people who did not believe in God, but who worshipped idols and different sorts of gods.'

'I know what "pagan" means,' I protested huffily.

'Ah! My very sincere apologies. I didn't mean to imply that you were ill-informed.'

I closed the drawer on St Patrick. All this baffling new knowledge was prompting even wider questions.

'If there were only Jews and pagans, and if some of the Jews became Christians, why didn't the rest of them try to turn the pagans into Jews? To make up for the ones they had lost.'

'Ah!' my father exclaimed proudly as he lit a fresh cigarette, 'that's a very intelligent question, my boy, which I shall endeavour to answer. Briefly, the early Christians believed that their religion was better than Judaism, that it was the only true faith, and so they considered it their duty to persuade as many others as possible to join them.'

'You mean, to convert them? There's a box in the lunch room at school for us to put pennies in to pay for the African Missions – they're Catholic priests who go out to Africa to convert the savages.'

'I don't think we should call them savages, son. Primitives, perhaps, but that's not the same as savages. However, to continue: the Jews considered themselves the children of God. Why? Well, the story is that before any of the peoples of the earth believed in God, He asked all the different tribes, one by one, to accept His Word and live by it forever. One by one they all refused, until He asked the Jews. They agreed. That's why we are called The Chosen People, though really it should be the other way round. We should be called The Choosing People, shouldn't we?'

My father hesitated and looked at me keenly, expecting me

to laugh or at least show some appreciation of his wit, but I was
too engrossed in his explanation to be amused.

'Anyway,' he went on, 'the Jews probably felt that since the
people with no religion had already rejected God's Word when
He offered it to them, there was no point in anyone else trying to
convince them. Besides, we believe that everyone has the right to
find his own path to God. So we don't try to convert people.'

Before I had time to consider this piece of information, I heard
a voice from the factory call, 'Boss! Boss! I'm here!' It was Hallisey.

Hallisey was my father's carrier, but the truth of the matter
was that most of the carrying was done by my father and by Jessy,
Hallisey's horse. My father always said that Hallisey was the bane
of his life, but I liked him. I think my father did, too.

He was a small man who looked like what I imagined a land-
pirate would look like. He wore a filthy sack around his middle,
and on his head was an equally filthy cap, but at such a rakish
angle that it perfectly complemented the cheeky glint in his eyes.
He was perpetually unshaven, his cheeks and chin mottled with
clusters of black spots – though how much was stubble and how
much plain dirt it was hard to say. Jessy, his horse, was not unlike
him. There was the same untidy forelock trying to stray down between the eyes, the same scanty acquaintance with soap and water,
the same emaciated appearance.

It was the emaciated appearance that caused the running
argument between my father and Hallisey.

'Look at her bones, just look at them,' my father used to protest. 'For God's sake, man, don't you ever feed the poor animal?'

''Pon me soul, boss,' Hallisey would answer, crossing himself
in the place where his heart was supposed to be, 'but that creature
eats as much as I do meself!'

'I can well believe that, Hallisey, for you're only a bundle of
skin and bones at best. But the poor horse works a good deal harder than you do. *You* don't need much more than a pint and a sand-
wich inside you to sit up on top of the cart cracking your whip.

But it's the horse does the pulling. I keep telling you to feed her properly.'

Such exchanges made my father unhappy. He often reminded me that the Bible said a man should attend to his animal's needs before he attended to his own, and time and again he tried to persuade Hallisey to take his responsibilities more seriously. Hallisey, however, while crossing himself devoutly and swearing to the Blessed Virgin that Jessy was fed three times a day, never mended his ways, and the horse's bones always stuck out through her skin.

Suddenly someone shouted my father's name and one of the neighbours' little children rushed panting in.

'Sir, sir, Mr Hallisey's horse is dyin', it's fallen down flat in the Main Street and Mr Hallisey can't get it up, it's dyin'.'

The words were almost incomprehensible, so madly did they tumble over themselves in the lad's excitement. 'I knew it,' my father groaned. 'I knew it. I knew it would happen some day. That animal is so under-nourished, goodness knows what disease has struck it down.'

Quickly clamping his hat on his head he ran out of the factory, myself and the messenger of ill-tidings on his heels.

Immediately he turned into North Main Street there were so many spectators gathered in the road that traffic had come to a standstill and he had to push his way through to get anywhere near the patient. He found the report had not been exaggerated. The shafts of the cart had been unbuckled and Jessy was stretched out on the road with a burly youth half-kneeling on her head. Beside him sat Hallisey, reclining on an armchair he had pulled off the cart, calmly tendering advice and instructions.

'The poor beast! The poor sufferin' animal!' he wailed, springing up the moment he saw my father. 'What misfortune is it has fallen on her, I wonder?'

'What indeed!' my father echoed. 'And by the same token, what misfortune is it that told that big oaf to sit on top of her head and crush the last of the life out of her?'

'But, sure that's only for the safety of the public, boss,' Hallisey protested, turning to the crowd as if inviting gratitude for his thoughtfulness and consideration, 'you know, if the beast kind of jumped up any way sudden and lashed out with those hooves.'

The rest of the sentence trailed away as my father very slowly paced a few circles around Jessy, examining her from every angle. The murmurs of the crowd subsided, apart from one woman who kept insisting that the vet should be sent for.

'Don't move,' my father ordered Hallisey after a moment. Then he turned and pushed his way back through the spectators. They parted for him as if he had been Moses parting the waters of the Red Sea. Within a minute he returned – carrying in his arms a bulging bag of oats. Carefully he placed the bag on the road beside the prostrate animal.

'Now, get up,' he ordered the youth holding the horse's head.

The youth got up.

So did Jessy. With a jingle of harness and a bound that would have done credit to a two-year old, she sprang to her feet and dug her nose into the bag.

A long wail, like a siren running down, escaped from the onlookers, and my father turned angrily to Hallisey.

'Did you give the animal any breakfast this morning?' he demanded.

'Breakfast, boss? Sure she has that every morning!'

'But *this* morning, Hallisey, *this* morning? Are you sure you fed her *this* morning?'

Hallisey frowned, as if to remember so far back required a tremendous effort of concentration. Then the answer hit him.

'Ah, of course, boss, that's right. I was in such a hurry to get to work that I must have forgot it. Yes, that's it – I must have forgot.'

My father grunted scornfully. 'You forgot all right. But Jessy didn't – and she just decided to go on strike until someone remembered. Look at her now!'

They both stood gazing at Jessy as she continued to eat her way into the bag of oats.

'Come along, son,' my father said, taking my hand. 'We must be getting back.'

As we reached the corner of the street we turned for a last look and saw that a policeman had appeared on the scene. He seemed to be questioning Hallisey closely, with the crowd milling around to hear what was being said. I thought my father would go back to explain what had happened, but he didn't.

'Is the policeman going to arrest Hallisey?' I asked him.

'I doubt it,' he said. 'He might summons him. That would mean Hallisey would have to appear in court, before a judge. The judge would hear the case, and if Hallisey was found guilty of neglecting Jessy, the judge would probably make him pay a fine.'

'How much?'

'Not a great deal. A few pounds or so.'

'But would Hallisey have money to pay?'

'Probably not.'

'Would they put him in jail then?'

'No. I'd pay the fine for him. If I didn't, he'd have to borrow from someone and that would mean he'd have even less money to buy food for Jessy.'

'You see, my son,' – we were back in my father's office now, and as he spoke, the smoke from his cigarette spurted from his mouth in little jets the way Jessy's breath had shot from her nostrils when she jumped up and started to eat her oats – 'it's just a matter of doing as much good as you can. That's really all God wants of us. To be good. A long time ago, in the time of the Bible, there was a famous Jewish sage – a wise man – who was asked to sum up the Jewish faith while he stood on one foot. That meant he had to be quick about it and hadn't any time for long explanations – unlike your father. His answer was: "Do not unto others as you would not have others do unto you. That is the Law. The rest is commentary." Do you understand that?'

'Of course,' I answered. 'It's easy.'

'Ah yes, easy to understand, but not always easy to remember. A man is judged by what he does, my boy, and what he does depends on what he believes.'

'I'd never change my religion,' I said. 'You wouldn't either, would you, Daddy?'

My father put his head on one side and scratched a while at his chin as if he suddenly had an old man's beard and was giving the question serious consideration.

'I might,' he answered, 'I might.'

I looked at him in horror and consternation. It couldn't be! Surely it couldn't be!

'But what would you change to?'

My voice was almost a whisper.

'A better Jew, my son. A better Jew,' and his booming laughter filled the office as my world fell into place again.

Catch as Cats Can

With Aaron and Catherine retiring to his home for their tête-à-tête lunch with Catherine cooking the food, Aaron dispensing further information from his Jew-town memories and hopefully the pair of them indulging in a get-to-know-you chat led probably by Catherine – Aaron too old and old-fashioned to ply her with personal questions unless encouraged – I was glad to have the opportunity of getting lunch for the most important cared for member of my family, our cat. Of course like all pets, cats are categorised – pun not intended – as animals, and therefore non-human, soulless. I suspect that if a poll were held of all pet-lovers, the vast majority in favour of 'human animals' would win hands down and hands up, triumphantly patting heads, shaking paws, and admiring wagging tails.

After all, it is said that a dog is a man's best friend, and far more often than not that is so. A dog that loves its owner never renounces that love, though I have heard that sometimes a pet dog lodged in a pound while its owner has to be away, needs some time to banish the fear of another such confinement and recover fully its trust in and love for its owner when that owner returns. Between human beings, however, the love sworn by wives or husbands or partners so frequently ends up transferred to other acquaintances. Cats, one must acknowledge, are by nature independent creatures that offer you a spell of smooch only when they are hungry or you are tickling them exactly where you know they want to be tickled. But they do have a innate intelligence, though unfortunately their human characteristics frequently render them too lazy or too sleepy to use it.

When I was in my early teens, a cat suddenly turned up in my home in Cork. I don't think any of my brothers or sister actually brought it in or even allowed it in, so maybe it just took advantage of some open door. There had never been any species of pet animal in the house and I had never thought I wanted one, but the intruder immediately won me over. It was so small and young-seeming that it couldn't have long been out of its kittenhood, but even so it was full of unfailingly kittenish buoyancy. What, however, completely fascinated me was its colour: it was black throughout. I don't know why its colour had such an effect on me. I knew that blackness resulted from a total absence of light, and indeed if at that particular period of my life I might happen to be out alone late at night, street darkness would make me hurry towards the lights of home.

As it had no identification I took it on myself to name it. I had good reason for my choice: that was the time of my first most rapturous Beethoven period, so Beethoven it was. The cat could hardly be said to have looked at all like the composer – a lion's head would have been the nearest to him – but calling it Beethoven meant that two creatures, a man and an animal, had begun to rent more than just a corner of my mind.

Unfortunately, the cat's visit was extremely short-lived. When my father arrived home, his immediate question was, 'Who brought that cat in?'

My honest answer was, 'No one did. It just came in of its own accord.'

'Well, whether it came in through a door or a window or down the chimney it's not ours, so put it out in the front and it will find its own way home. Cats always know where their home is. Do it now before it gets used to you or you to it. Go on.'

So I went on, not surprised at my father's banishment of Beethoven as he had never had any sort of animal in the house, but I was also surprised by the quite reasonable tone and terms of his order. I would have expected that he might well have displayed ailurophobic characteristics, but there was no evidence of that in his behaviour. On the other hand, I can claim that *my* behaviour was clearly that of an ailurophile. To set the matter straight however, I must admit that I hadn't then the slightest idea what either word meant, and it took me some years even to learn of their existence and to find out, with some self-satisfied pride, that I was an ailurophile myself.

The cat that made me one was christened Sappho by my wife, Ita, when we moved into our first house. Writing about it now, I reminded myself of the discovery by Aaron's parents when they arrived from Lithuania to Jewtown and found on the first night they rented their tiny, squeezed Eastville home that the house was infested by bugs. It wasn't by bugs that our new residence was infested, but by mice, these underground, night-raiding rodents that made employment of a cat essential. Fortunately, that presented no difficulty because my mother-in-law, who lived near us, had a female cat that was frequently impregnated by a neighbouring, marauding Siamese, and so my wife was allowed her choice of its latest litter. The original Sappho was a Greek poet, born about 612 BC, about whose life not a great deal is known, but her poetry – hymns to the gods, marriage-songs and love poems – has won for her a place among the great poets of all time.

Our Siamese cross-breed Sappho with fawn-coloured short hair, a narrow head and blue eyes, was about a month old when she became ill. We immediately took her to the vet, who after his examination was able to tell us that she had a touch of cat flu. He dosed her and gave us enough medication to administer to Sappho two drops of the tincture every two hours throughout that night and the next day. Her recovery followed very speedily, but even so, misfortune caught up with her. Some time afterwards, early one evening a knock at our door brought a near neighbour who said that a cat was lying by the footpath outside our house, having been hit by a motorcyclist. Was the cat ours? Indeed it was Sappho, alive, but unable to move. As carefully as possible we lifted her onto a board and brought her indoors. We phoned the vet, who arrived very quickly, and found that she had sustained some bone fracture to her spine. He would take her to his surgery immediately, do the best he could to ascertain if the fracture would knit, and would let us know the outcome as soon as possible. I don't remember how long we had to wait for his verdict, but when it did come, we learned that the fracture was too serious and Sappho would have to be put down.

Her death so soon after she had come to us was something we had to bear, and though putting her down had been humane, thinking how in her short life she had suffered illness, and having recovered had then met with a cruel end, was doubly distressful. More, what we also lost was sufficient time to bond completely with out first cat.

Because we needed both to drown our sorrow and to replace without delay our mice vigilante, we once again had recourse to my mother-in-law's family of cats and gladly took another of her Siamese cross-breeds. As on the previous occasion, her father was the local Siamese philanderer, while its mother was the producer of Sappho in an earlier litter, thus making Sappho and her successor full sisters. Not, we hoped, an ill-fated choice.

Our new cat was quite a beauty. Apart from her face she was almost white at first, gradually shading to somewhat darker than pale fawn but retaining the cream hue on her belly and chest. Her dark face also had a cream patch between her ears, set off by sparkling blue eyes and four white paws. And as I hadn't had the privilege of christening Sappho, I claimed the right to name our new cat. I called her Vashti.

In the Hebrew lessons of my youth I came across the name, and in later life I learned rather more about its bearer than *Cheder* lessons revealed. Vashti was a Persian queen, the wife of King Ahasuerus.

There is a story in the book of Esther that once, when the king was rather more than three-sheets-in-the-wind, he ordered Vashti to appear before his assembled nobles wearing her royal crown so as to show off her charms. In the Talmud, the Rabbis' interpretation of the order was that she was to wear her crown and nothing else. Vashti refused, as a result of which the king's advisers, in what must have been an angry combination of chagrin and dudgeon, told him he should depose her so that her refusal would not encourage other women to defy their husbands. Ahasuerus followed the advice and deposed Vashti, whose removal paved the way for Queen Esther. Vashti, however, found her fame when, in the emergence of Jewish feminism in the second half of the 1900s, she was lauded as its earliest heroine.

Our Vashti certainly needed no crown to embellish her cat charms and she quickly grew into a real beauty. We found that she was ever ready to be played with and rubbed, and a day arrived when with a bound she suddenly landed on my shoulder, since when she was happy to settle there wherever I moved inside the house. Such behaviour amazed me. Why did she do it, I wondered. Was it that the body-contact appealed to her? But how could a bony, male shoulder be comfortable to a cat? What matter, for I allowed myself to believe that she had confirmed the existence of a special bond between us. And the fact, as I later discovered, that many Siamese cats have a preference for such a conveyance did not for a single moment discommode me. Vashti and I, I felt, were a pair.

As time went on, during which we were more a trio than a pair – my wife having always considered Vashti as special as I did – the trio was expanded into a quartet by the arrival of our daughter, Sarah. As she grew up into childhood, not surprisingly Vashti became a playmate for her, until one day she missed her. For the first time Vashti had disappeared.

It was on an Easter weekend, Good Friday evening, that she failed to come home and be fed. We presumed she would surely

turn up on Easter Saturday. She didn't. On the Saturday morning
I spent some time in our back garden, calling her in the hope that
somehow she might be in one of any of the gardens that bounded
us on both sides and were each longer than a cricket pitch, as indeed our own was. There was no response. Nor on the Sunday
morning. However, I went out to the garden again in the afternoon, for I wouldn't give up. The air was very still and particularly quiet – we knew that many of our near neighbours were away
for all of the weekend. In that outdoor silence I suddenly thought
I might have heard some unusual sound. Soft. Not a human call.
I listened again, rigid, so that not even my own muscle-movement
should whisper. Was it a cat's appeal? Was it Vashti? If so, why was
it so weak? I made a guess. Was she locked in somewhere? Two
gardens away there was a high, specially built brick shed the whole
garden's length in which its owner stored boxes of goods in which
he dealt. I knew he was away for Easter, but how would I get into
his garden to see into his shed? There was a fence between ours
and our next door neighbour's, concealed by a row of tall trees.
Somehow I found one narrow gap in the fence, forced myself
through it and between two tree trunks. I ran across to the equally
strongly prepared fence of the shed owner's garden. There was no
way through or over it, but while I was able to see the shed windows, they were so begrimed that even if Vashti was locked in
there, it would be impossible to discern her. If? There was no if. I
heard a cat meowing. It wasn't the shed owner's, he didn't have
one. It had to be Vashti.

I knew no one would be back until late on Monday evening
or, worse still, not until Tuesday morning, so all I could do was
leave a note in the owner's letterbox. I wrote 'Our cat is locked in
your shed. No matter how late it may be when you come home,
don't try to let her out as she may run away. Even if I'm in bed,
please knock at our door and I'll get up immediately and take care
of her.' I was greatly afraid that if Vashti was faced by a stranger,
she might well be so scared that she'd just rush past him and then

goodness knows where she might flee.

In the early hours of Monday morning there was a loud knocking on our front door. I put on a dressing gown and slippers, opened the door to the neighbour who told me that Vashti was in his shed, that he tried to catch her so as to bring her to me, but she ran away from him. He took me to the shed, which was all lit up, and there, crouched right under the high roof on one of a pillar of boxes, was Vashti. I called her. There was no way to climb up to her, so I asked the shed owner to bring me a saucer of milk. He left to get it. Once he was gone, Vashti made her way down a few boxes, and once she was in reach of me she leaped right into my arms. As the neighbour returned with the saucer of milk, I had already made my way out, firmly cradling Vashti. I declined the milk, explaining she'd be happier if I got her back home quickly to her familiar surroundings. The scene that followed was like the last moments of a tear-squeezing Hollywood film ending – two embracing companions, one whispering assurances and the other purring relief, both going home to the applauding audience of wife and daughter.

Vashti's normal routine resumed with, however, a somewhat unique experiment of mine. Yes, she was a cat, not a dog, but I had begun to believe that many animals, particularly domestic ones, could actually talk. That is not to say that it could talk to you, but that you could talk to it. Saying what? Well, dogs, for instance, can be trained to respond to certain orders and sounds. Your voice, which projects your language both in tone and choice of special words, is what a dog learns to understand and submit to. It will submit because it uses its intelligence, just as a human listener who during its childhood and education will have achieved its own sufficiently developed intelligence, will be able to respond with acts or words. Trained sheepdogs follow exactly the farmer's different whistles as to how to corral a herd of sheep. A pet dog, out for a walk with its owner, will rush to fulfil his or her call instead of delaying to make use of almost every tree; and whether out or in, will 'sit' when it has learned what the word, sometimes accompanied by a pointed sign, means. Why ever then should it not be possible to teach Vashti by word and finger pointing to sit on the rug in front of me when I am in a chair and she has been one way or another trying to disturb me.

It took time, but with voice, tone, directional signs and even some amateurish semi-gymnastic assistance, Vashti eventually learned that 'Sit' meant 'Sit down on the rug and be quiet'. I had succeeded and so had she. Perhaps not on every occasion – there was, after all, the odd time when she refused with a four-footed stand-up attitude and an angry stare in her eyes that was her un-ladylike way of saying, 'Bugger off, you'.

As our household royal cat, our Queen Vashti was never de-posed. She was treasured by me, my wife, and our daughter, and she was completely happy with us for many further years. That is, until she disappeared once more, not this time into her neigh-bour's shed – she was clearly too intelligent to ever go near that prison again – but where was she? The fearful, four-letter, pet-applicable word 'lost' was avoided, but the even more terrifying 'dead', and lying in some roadside gutter as Sappho had suffered, tormented all our thoughts. Ita and I scoured every district near and as possible far, and put 'lost' messages in as many shop win-dows as we could, but no news, good or bad, reached us. By then a week had passed and we feared, indeed reluctantly supposed, the worst.

At the end of that night I, not yet asleep, heard what seemed to be weak cat-calls from a downstairs room. I went down to investigate. If there was a cat, how could it have got in? All doors were closed and no cat had come in through the garden cat-flap door. There came another cry, clearly from the small room front-ing the garden. I went in, in my haste and in the dark not even switching on the light because I immediately saw in the darkness a black shape on the ledge outside the locked window. I opened the window. A cat sat there, but the night was so dark that I couldn't possibly be sure if it was Vashti. I lifted it into my arms and took it out to the lit corridor. It was Vashti, it was Vashti. I rushed up to our bedroom, put her on the bed, and we all had a family celebration. Where had she been for so long? Her paw pads were all very hot – did that mean she had come from a long distance? Perhaps she had inadvertently got herself locked in the boot of a car that had gone on a journey very many miles away from Dublin, and when she was released it took her all of a week to find her way home through perhaps tenebrous fields and snarling streets. Whatever the explanation was, it didn't matter now. We gave her milk and a little food, and put her to bed. Next day she was as happy as if she had been away on a holiday and had brought back with her the gift of her eager affection.

I don't know exactly how old she was at that time – maybe ten or so – but some four years later she began to appear not to be in her usual active good spirits. We took her to the vet, whose examination revealed that her system was showing some signs of beginning to fail. A regular steroid injection might cure her, but we would have to bring her in for a further injection every month. We did so, but it was not too long before we found ourselves making what became our last mercy journey. The vet quietly told us that the quality of life for Vashti was such that the only thing to do was to save her further misery and put her down. We knew there was no alternative. I turned to my wife and we both nodded.

'Please keep her still,' the vet said to me.

I put one hand on her head and the other on her back.

'Sit, Vashti,' I whispered, 'sit.'

In a split second she went completely limp.

I broke down.

We took her home and waited for Sarah to come from school so she could say goodbye to Vashti and be with us for her burial. We dug a grave in the garden, laid her down on a small rug on which she had liked to sleep, put her food bowl beside her, and covered her grave. On it Sarah planted a flower.

A few years ago, Kevin Myers of the *Irish Times* wrote about the death of his pet dog, Traffic: 'Traffic is dead,' he said, 'and my life will never be quite the same again. We had him put down on Tuesday. Death took him totally, as death does; but its utter totality is always astonishing. The body remains, but Traffic is gone, and just as conclusively, something precious and irreplaceable has vanished from my life, and for all time.'

I understood exactly how he felt.

Our new cat, after Vashti's death, was just an ordinary kitten, given to us by a neighbour. She was all black and attractive, and Sarah was given the right to name her. Sarah was then a fan of Wimbledon tennis, and was particularly amused by an American women's singles contender. What amused her was that this entrant, who was black, whenever she bent forward to take her opponent's service, wiggled her bottom, exactly as our new kitten herself often did. Not that the latter watched the tennis and copied the player, but the American unfortunately didn't get very far in the tournament. She was Zina Garrison, and so Sarah named the kitten 'Zena'.

Zena grew up without any troubles, though she severely rationed her gifts of affection. Early in life she had begun to spend most of each day in our back garden, but it was suddenly invaded by a male cat, named Chip, who hailed from a neighbour directly behind us. Zena had already been spayed, and in fact Chip was never particularly interested in her, but she didn't half resent his presence in what was her territory. She screamed, hissed and spat her warnings so much that Chip kept his distance. The tragedy was that Zena was immediately possessed by an intense fear of him that has never left her. When she comes in from the garden, she runs halfway up the stairs and pushes her head through the banister from where she can keep a watch through the upper glass panels of the back door for Chip's appearance. Sometimes when she is lazing in the garden and Chip, in quite a friendly manner, approaches her, the sparks fly, Chip speedily fleeing from her threatening claws. Such small victories brought no balm to Zena's nerves, and she became obsessed by her fear. Since then nothing has changed.

Doubtless not all cats go through their lives with no particular untoward troubles, and in the nature of things no sensible cat owner would take it for granted that his or her pet has a guardian angel guaranteeing its completely assured lifeline, but to have three cats, one after another like Sappho, killed on the road, Vashti having to be put down, and now Zena, unnecessarily feeling scared day and night by an unthreatening Chip, might seem to an ailurophile a rather bad run. Not so – it is the cats who have had the bad run. I, on the other hand, have been lucky for some thirty years to live with and learn from three friends who, alas, are widely rated along with their breed as non-human, soulless citizens.

Past Tense

'Everything going well, Catherine?' Aaron asked as he poked his head into the kitchen, 'I'm not complaining, just making sure you're not finding any difficulties with the kitchen.'

'All's well, Aaron. The kitchen is really perfect. No comparison with what I have in my one-room flat! Now just sit back and relax. The spuds are nearly ready – that's all we're waiting for.'

'There's a lovely smell in here anyway and I'm looking forward to our lunch. I'll leave you to it.'

Aaron went back to his chair and relaxed, as ordered. It made him remember how his wife had cooked such wonderful dishes for him in their first kitchen, even though that kitchen wasn't anything like the one he had now. So many years had passed since he last thought of it. She had often said to him, 'My man, your wife is queen of the kitchen, so you keep out of it.' There was a queen in his kitchen now, and he felt upset that Catherine seemed to have only one room to live in. What a way for a girl to live.

He looked at the table. She had set it in a jiffy before she even commenced the cooking. Two places – yes, another memory. He rested his head on the back of the chair and closed his eyes. He had seldom thought about the past these days, even these years. It was all gone, long, long ago. All he had now was the present – and damn little future.

He heard Catherine making her entry and quickly rose to help her.

'Now I hope you like it,' she said as she sat down. 'I haven't made any starter, just one main course, chicken, spuds and veg. I do hope it's OK and that you eat chicken. I thought you wouldn't eat meat because it wouldn't be *kosher*. That's the right word, isn't it? I looked it up, and of course there's no Jewish butcher in Cork now.'

'Catherine, what you've put in front of me is perfect, so don't worry. And as regards a Jewish butcher in Cork, what we did have many years ago was a non-Jewish *kosher* butcher.'

'A non-Jewish *kosher* butcher?' Catherine exclaimed. 'How in the world was that possible!'

'I remember him well,' Aaron said. 'A very nice man. Jones was his name, he had his butcher shop in – oh, I forget the name of the street and the *kosher* meat would come down to him from the Jewish community in Dublin one particular day every week. Mr Jones used shut his shop except to the Cork Jews, I think it might have been for just every Friday morning only. Our minister would see that everything was properly prepared, and a member of the community would do the carving with special knives that were kept for it. That's how it was done, year after year.'

'And what about Dublin? Was there a big community there, and how well were they served?'

'It used to be big. In the early 1900s there would have been the best part of two and a half thousand Jews in Dublin. It kept going up for years, but by 1990 it was down to about fifteen hundred. I don't know what it's down to by now and I imagine it has lost most, if not all, of the Jewish delicatessen shops. Though they might still have a *kosher* butcher.'

Catherine shook her head.

'Why are you shaking your head?' Aaron asked.

'Well, it's such a funny – no, a horrible world these days, so I'm wondering whether some day there'll be no Jews left in Dublin, they'll be down to just one, like Cork is. Well, if they do go down to one, I hope their last one is as good a person as you.'

'Thank you for your kind words, Catherine. It's been a very long time since ... no, no point in going on about me.'

'Well, let's not be worrying about depressing things. Tell me more about the Cork Jews' story. But first, if you're ready, I'll get our dessert. Some nice apple tart, and coffee or tea, whatever you prefer.'

Aaron shook his head as if he was saying no. Shaking his head from side to side was just his way of expressing his good fortune at how she was treating him. He almost felt too overcome to say yes. Eventually he found the word.

'Yes, my girl, my wonder girl, yes. Tart and tea. That would be lovely. And then we'll talk again.'

Catherine took only a minute or two to bring in the dessert, having had the tart ready and needing only to re-boil the kettle.

'Marvellous,' Aaron said, 'just marvellous.'

'Good,' said Catherine as she sat down. 'Now, continue with your story.'

'Well, while you were in the kitchen I remembered there once was some speculation that around 1694 there was a Jewish community in Cork, but evidently nothing about it was known. However, exactly one hundred years later there was in Cork a community of Sephardi Jews who traded in the import and export of *kosher* meat to the West Indies and the North American colonies. It was a very small community – Sephardi Jews are descendants of Spanish Jewry, while the other group, the Ashkenazim, are descended from German Jewry. The leader of the Sephardim in Cork had a son, Isaac Solomon, who was apprenticed to the goldsmith and silversmith trades, and he became one of Cork's great silver craftsmen whose work, it seems, is still sought after.'

'My goodness, over two hundred years ago, I bet if you could get any work of his now, it would be worth a pretty penny.'

'I wonder how long will that phrase "A pretty penny" last?' Aaron said with a laugh. 'We've had the euro for a long time already, haven't we?'

'We have indeed. And what about "A penny for your thoughts?" Can you imagine "A euro for your thoughts"?'

They both laughed, particularly Aaron.

'Well done, Catherine. Your smartness has given me the best laugh for ages. A very valuable pennyworth, my dear.'

'Stop, stop, Aaron, or I'll choke over my last bit of tart. I think we'd better go back to where we were.'

'Very good then. Is there anything special in your mind?'

'Well, yes. You told me about the friendship between them all in Jewtown, the Jews and the Catholics, over a hundred years ago, and I've been wondering whether there has ever been any pogrom in Cork. I know about the one in Limerick, in 1904. It always seems to get written about, but we've never heard about any trouble like that in Cork.'

Aaron closed his eyes for nearly a minute, almost as if he was praying. When he opened them again, he nodded, and started to explain.

'Firstly, as to the word "pogrom". It's a Yiddish word – that's a different language from Hebrew – and in fact it comes from Russian, meaning "a devastation". In the Limerick pogrom in 1904 there was no devastation, in the usual sense of the word. What took place was some violence and injuries too, abuse and stone-throwing. Worse was an almost total boycott of Jewish trades and business people, incited by a Redemptorist priest. And just as bad, maybe even worse, was the refusal of Jews in almost all shops. The whole affair went on for many months and resulted in the departure from Limerick of almost every Jewish family, some of whom ended up in Cork.

'Now, as to Cork. Well before the Limerick trouble in 1904, there were two anti-Jewish incidents in Cork. One never hears about them because, really, "incidents" is all they could be called. The first one was in 1888 when some members of a local trades council made anti-Jewish comments. As a result, the Mayor of Cork, John O'Brien, sent a long letter to the *Times* of London, in the course of which he wrote, "Irishmen are proud of the fact that theirs is the only country in Europe in which Jews have never been persecuted …"

'The second incident occurred in 1894 and apparently there were some attacks on the homes of Jewish residents. The two leading Home Rulers of the day, John Redmond and Justin Mc-Carthy, sent letters of protest to the M.P., Samuel Montague, in which the former stated that the attacks were "Consequent upon the inauguration of the system of street preaching", and Justin McCarthy's letter ended with what I thought were very well-chosen, indeed striking words: "Our Irish national poet, Thomas Moore, has again and again drawn comparisons between the persecution of the Irish race and that of the 'Sad One of Zion'." So, as you can see, as far as anti-Jewish trouble is concerned, Cork has virtually a clean slate.'

'Yes, I'm delighted to learn that. It'll be extremely important to include it in my story so that the *Examiner* readers can be proud of our city. But on the other hand –' Suddenly she stopped.

'What were you about to say?' Aaron questioned. 'On the other hand what?'

'Oh, it was just silly. Just that Cork's slate will stay clean forever because –' She stopped again.

'Catherine, don't be afraid of saying it. You were thinking that when I'm gone, there'll be no Jews in Cork for anyone to get to know them, live with them and see that they're basically just ordinary people. Wasn't that it?'

'Yes, in a way that was exactly it. The absence of Jews will be, already has been, Cork's loss. Oh, let's talk about something else. First I'll clear the dishes and things. Your dishwasher will do them.'

Catherine went towards the kitchen and Aaron noticed that for a moment she paused to look at his wedding photograph. He waited until she returned.

'Why did you stop to look at that picture, my dear? You must

have had something about it in your mind. We know each other
well enough by now to be quite open between us. Do you agree?'

Catherine nodded. 'Yes, I do, I do. I never thought that someone like me, and an orphan too, could in only a few days feel so
at ease with a man of ninety – give or take a couple of days.'

They both laughed at her added-on phrase.

'You know, my dear,' Aaron said, 'you might be surprised if I
tell you that I feel just as warm and grateful for such a – you might
call it a whirlwind – close relationship as ours. And indeed you
have just given me a second reason for my feelings. You see Catherine, like you I am an orphan too, hardly because I'm nearly
ninety, but because I was only six when both my parents died.'

'Only six! And both your parents died! You were living at
Eastville then. Oh Aaron, it must have been terrible for you.'

'No, in fact it wasn't so terrible for me, not then. My father
and mother had gone over to London and while they were there,
they both got the flu – there was a big epidemic around the time
the Great War ended – and neither of them survived. They died
within a day of each other.'

'Oh Aaron,' Catherine cried, 'don't tell me if it's too much
for you.'

'Thank you, thank you. It's not too much for me. I want to
tell it to you, I've never had anyone I could tell it to before. Not
even my wife. But I can tell it now. Not having had my parents
for eighty-four years after I was only six, it's almost as if I never
had any parents at all. So please let me tell it.'

'Yes, of course do.'

'Well,' Aaron started, 'in one way there's next to nothing I
know about my parents, about their lives or their death. I was a
very quiet boy, very self-contained, not talkative. I picked up English easily from the Christian people around Jewtown, playing
with their children there. My parents picked it up too, though not
as easily as I did. Mostly they spoke Yiddish to each other. I didn't
know they were going to London until a day before they left.

They didn't tell me why they were going and I didn't ask them, probably because they said they'd be back very quickly. They asked our next-door neighbours, Jewish of course, if they'd take me in for a while, and of course they did. Naturally, in Jewtown a Jewish family helped each other without question whenever help was needed. So I lived with our neighbours – they had two children, both girls, young girls – too old to play with me or I with them.

'Then I began to wonder why my parents hadn't yet come back. They had told me they wouldn't be very long, but already over a week had passed and I was still with my neighbours. I didn't ask then when my parents would return, because I was always too shy to ask any questions and I was afraid that if I asked them, they might think I wasn't happy being with them or didn't like them. But when another week passed and I was still alone, I just had to say something. So I thought the most mannerly question would be, "Will my mother and father be back tomorrow?" and that's what I said. They looked at each other – would you believe, I knew their names then, but as I seldom addressed them, I've forgotten their names long ago. They seemed embarrassed, didn't know what to say, but then the woman said to her man, "Tell him, Misha, tell him. We have to." My goodness, that's his name, Misha. It has come back to me suddenly, just because I'm talking about my parents.

'So anyway, he took me up and put me on his knee, and he said, "Aaron, I'm sorry, they can't come back." "They can't come back? Why?" I asked. He paused, then blew his nose. "They died, Aaron, they both died. They caught the flu and they died. We had a letter from a nurse in the hospital there over a week ago. We're so sorry, *mein kinde*, so sorry. But you'll live with us now. We'll always take care of you."

'That's the whole conversation. I've always remembered everything he said. At that time I knew nothing about death and burials, but a few years later I was old enough to ask why weren't my parents buried in Cork, and Misha explained that to bring them back to Cork, he would have needed money he didn't have. It would have cost so much – it embarrassed him to have to tell me – and anyway it seems the hospital had to bury them very quickly after they died. I suppose when I had grown up, if I had done something about finding out the name and address of the hospital, they might have been able to tell me where their graves were. But I didn't. There was so little I ever knew about them and I was so young when I last saw them, that I hardly remember what they looked like, and they never had their photograph taken. Certainly, never in Lithuania. It wasn't till I had grown up that I began to really wonder about them.'

Catherine lifted the teapot and held it over Aaron's cup. He smiled and nodded.

'But what made you begin to wonder about your parents? I mean, you had known next to nothing about them, so what was it that passed through your mind?'

'As you said, I knew next to nothing about them, including why did they suddenly go to London. That's really what I wondered about. I could have asked Misha, but he may not have known why, they might not have told him. And even if they did know the reason, it may have been something he couldn't tell me or didn't want to. By that time Misha had a tailoring business and I was his apprentice. So I felt shy about trying to talk to him about my parents. What I would have wanted to ask him, what I was wondering about, was something that would have embarrassed me, and probably him too.'

'Don't tell me if you don't want to,' Catherine said quietly.

'I wouldn't be a bit embarrassed to tell you, my dear. You're not a man, as Misha was, and I was still an adolescent then. I'm a bit beyond that now. You're a woman, so you'd understand. Not that what I was wondering about was in any way something unpleasant or unnatural.'

'I wouldn't have imagined it could be, Aaron. So go ahead.'

'Well, it was just that in my teens, I began to wonder whether what took my parents to London was that my mother wanted to have another child, but for some reason, some difficulty, she needed expert advice and thought London was the place to get it. No doubt it was a hare-brained question to get into my mind, but what else could I wonder? I think what started me thinking it was the sisters, Misha's daughters. Oh no, not that they ever said a word to me – they were both some years older than me, and to them I was probably only still a child. They were, in fact, both very attractive and well brought up girls, and it was seeing so much of them made me wish I had a sister of my own. But I hadn't one – and I never would have. And that, just that, was what put it in my mind as the reason – the only but mad reason – that made me wonder if perhaps my mother was pregnant and if perhaps the local advice she got told her London was the only place where she might get the necessary help. Men are funny animals. Catherine, once that idea stuck in my mind, I was, sort of not happy, just satisfied. I could then put it in the back of my mind and get it permanently out of the front. What do you think of that?'

Catherine sat silently for a while, not really knowing what to say.

'It's difficult for you, isn't it?' Aaron asked.

'It is, I suppose. But the best thing about it is that at least you thinking about it when you did has put it well at the back of your mind. And I'm really glad that telling it all to me has, I hope, been a help too.'

'It has, my dear, and I'm deeply grateful. I think you deserve some rest after such a story. And some recompense too. So tomorrow's journey will be a pleasant trip to the Marina. No doubt you've been there, Catherine.'

'Yes, but not for years.'

'Nor have I. I know it has changed – or some of it has – but I imagine the river part of it should be as beautiful as it always was. And I have a special reason for wanting to go there, two special reasons in fact to tell you about.'

'Oh, I look forward to that, I really do. For the rest of this day, I'll wonder what they can be. But before I leave, I'll clear up what's on the table.'

'Be gone, young woman, be gone. I'm perfectly able to do them myself. So off with you, my dear.'

'Thank you, Aaron, and sleep well tonight.'

She put her arms around him and placed a quick, soft kiss on his cheek. Then she left. Aaron was too overcome to say even goodbye.

Voices Lost and Found

Certain Irish writers I had the privilege of publishing – those from whom there is a permanent absence of new work owing to their retirement from writing, or disappearance, or death – are always regarded by me as having been special, even if we never met.

Take, for instance, James Stern. How many Irish readers knew of James Stern's fame as one of the greatest short story writers in Britain, or much less even knew that he was, in fact, Irish? He was born in Kilcairne, Co. Meath, in 1904, his Jewish father being one of an Anglo-German banking family, his mother an Irish Protestant, the great love of fox-hunting having brought them together. Their home was The Abbey Farm in Bective, where they had twelve indoor and twenty outdoor servants, but they left it in 1926 to live in England. The estate was sold in that year to an American, who had been persuaded to buy it by his Roscommon-born friend, Tom Lavin. Tom had met Nora Mahon, from Athenry, in the US, and they married in 1911, their daughter, Mary, being born there in 1912.

In 1978 James Stern, writing in the *Irish Press* about his departure from Bective in 1926, said 'Did it really happen, or did I dream that on the day we drove away I dared to look back, and there, framed in the doorway, stood a girl of maybe ten?' That girl was of course Mary Lavin, whose parents had been installed to oversee the Bective estate for the new purchaser. In the early 1940s when Stern was in New York, he had read Mary Lavin's first collection of stories, *Tales From Bective Bridge*, published in 1943. Then in 1978 he reread the collection when Poolbeg Press reissued it in a first paperback edition for which Mary wrote a special introduction, and he reviewed it for the *Irish Press*. In it he said that he 'could think of no other living writer of stories whose first collection attains such maturity.' Twenty-five years after he left Bective he returned for the first time to Ireland and was welcomed to Bective by Mary Lavin. He remembered thinking at that time that he never felt so much at home – 'Glory be! What was I after saying! I *was* home!' He always yearned for Ireland, and as he put it, he 'could recognise and name most of the wild flowers, ride a horse and milk a cow … the only places I could feel at home, where on arrival I am promptly overwhelmed by the human element, by the familiarity of sounds and smells, are Dublin and Paris.'

A number of his stories were set in Ireland or were about Irish characters living elsewhere, and many of them were autobiographical. From the 1950s on he apparently wrote few new stories, probably because he became a voluminous letter-writer to many other illustrious correspondents, including W. H. Auden, William Plomer, Samuel Beckett, Arthur Miller, Kay Boyle and Malcolm Lowry.

In 1948, he was awarded a prize for his short story writing by the American Academy of Letters, and in 1966 he was chosen by V. S. Pritchett for the first British Arts Council Award given to a writer of short stories.

James Stern, one of Ireland's great writers, but mostly unrecognised in his own country, died on 27 November 1993, aged eighty-eight.

What twentieth century Irish writer had his work compared by critics to Faulkner and Conrad? His name was James Hanley.

He was born in Dublin in 1901, his father being from Dublin, his mother from Cork. When I published him in *Irish Writing* in

March 1953, he told me that his real name was Hanly, but the 'e' had infiltrated after a long Northern England sojourn. What he probably didn't know was that 'Hanley' was the anglicised form of the Irish Ó hÁinle, thought to be from the Gaelic word *álainn*, meaning 'beautiful'.

His father became a merchant seaman and James followed in his footsteps by running away to Liverpool when he was thirteen. He joined a ship's crew and, after being many years as a deckhand he became variously a railway porter, butcher, cook, clerk, post-man and journalist. Then he started to write. His first novel was published in 1930 and was later followed by *The Furys*, his trilogy of Dublin slum life. The trilogy displayed his power of depicting horror and misery, and he became recognised as one of the most powerful of contemporary writers, which probably explains why eminent critics were often moved to lament the popular neglect of his work.

James Hanley died in November 1985. What chance is there that any of his books will be reissued? The answer is clear, and a great twentieth-century Irish writer will remain completely for-gotten.

'I don't know whether in Ireland she is considered an Irish writer or an American. In fact, she is both, and both countries ought to be proud to claim her.'

So wrote William Maxwell in 1933, the main short story editor of *The New Yorker*, and an Irish answer to him at that time would almost certainly have been: 'Who is this writer? Who in Ireland has ever read her, or has even heard of her?' The writer was Maeve Brennan, born in Dublin in 1917, she died in New York in 1993, aged seventy-six.

She lived in Dublin until she was seventeen when in 1934 her father, Robert Brennan, was appointed Ireland's ambassador to the United States, and the whole family moved to Washing-ton. At the end of Robert Brennan's tenure in 1947, he and his family returned to Ireland, but Maeve stayed in New York. She worked first as a copywriter for *Harper's Bazaar*, where her first short story was published in 1950, but in 1949 she joined the staff of *The New Yorker* in which all her subsequent stories appeared, her last one being in 1973. Her death in 1993 came after more than a decade of mental illness during which she frequently suffered psychotic episodes.

I first came across a Maeve Brennan story, 'The Springs of Affection', in *The New Yorker* in 1972 and for me it was one of the best short stories I had ever read. It was set in Ireland, and she was clearly Irish. The biographical note said that her first collection, *In and Out of Never-Never Land*, had been published in 1969. I visited every bookshop in Dublin, but not one had the book or had even heard of it or of the writer. I enquired from some source in the US and eventually was able to get a copy. It contained twenty-two stories, almost all of them Irish. I published one of the stories, 'The Carpet With The Big Pink Roses On It', in 'New Irish Writing' on 29 September 1973, and another one, 'Christmas Eve', on 22 December 1973. It became the title story of her second collection.

In 1973, Maeve Brennan returned to Dublin. I contacted her and asked her if she would have dinner with my wife and me in our home. She came, we had a pleasant evening, and when she was leaving she invited us to have lunch with her in the flat she had rented in Ballsbridge. My wife and I arrived at the right place and time, but when the front door was opened by a lady and we asked for Maeve Brennan, we were told that only a few days before, Maeve Brennan had without any warning upped and gone back to the US. When she died twenty years later and we read in the US obituaries of the frequently harrowing years of the final decades of her life, we presumed that her sudden departure from Dublin in 1973 must have happened during one of her psychotic episodes.

No other book of hers was published before her death, but in 2000 a suddenly discovered novella, entitled *The Visitor*, written in the 1940s and almost certainly her first book, was hailed as a twentieth-century classic, and confirmed the author's reputation as one of the best Irish short story writers since Joyce.

For me that whole story doesn't end quite there. When I learned about the amazing discovery of *The Visitor* manuscript, I began to think about its author and to feel that there was some connection with her, some relationship, that just would not surface. At last it came to me, another of those fifty-year old memories that had somehow reawakened. It was about Maeve Brennan's father, Robert Brennan, by whom I had published in the March 1952 edition of *Irish Writing* a story he wrote for me about his escape one day in 1921 from the Black and Tans. He was travelling on the top of one of the open-top trams which was stopped on Baggot Street Bridge by a party of Auxiliaries and khaki-clad soldiers. Brennan had in his pocket decoded messages for the underground Republican Government from their agent in Germany, and he knew that he had no hope of escaping with his life if the Auxiliaries searched him, which they certainly would do. Suddenly a passenger in a nearby seat whom he recognised as an American journalist he had met a few days before, moved beside him and asked 'Have you got anything on you?'

Brennan told him he had some papers. The journalist took them and put them in his pocket.

'I have an American passport,' he said. 'They won't search me.'

The Auxiliaries searched Brennan but not the journalist, and when the tram was allowed to move off, the journalist gave Brennan back his papers and got off at the next stop.

Perhaps the title of Maeve's novella, *The Visitor*, was what reminded me of her father's lucky escape from his unwelcome visitors on that day in 1921!

One Irish writer I cannot omit is Robert Gibbings. He was born in Cork in 1889 and educated at UCC, the Slade School and the

Central School of Arts, London. He studied medicine for two years before turning to art, but when the First World War broke out he joined the Royal Munster Fusiliers and was wounded in battle at Gallipoli. When he was demobbed in 1918 he started engraving, and then in 1924 he became the proprietor of the Golden Cockerel Press.

He was a widely experienced world traveller who became a highly-regarded travel writer, his books being illustrated with his own engravings, many of which are collected in the British Museum and in the Victoria and Albert Museum.

His first travel book, in 1936, was *Coconut Island*, but it was his third one, *Sweet Thames Run Softly*, published in 1940, that made his fame. In 1944 came *Lovely is the Lee* and in 1951 *Sweet Cork of Thee*. Altogether he wrote eleven books, and with his own illustrations they are prized by collectors. His eighth and last book happened, so fittingly, to be titled *Till I End My Song*, and was published very shortly before he died in 1958. The fiftieth anniversary of his death will be in January 2008, so there is plenty of time for Cork to prepare an exhibition of his books and engravings. Robert Gibbings deserves such honour from his art and literature lovers.

One of the greatest Irish poets I never published – because he wrote poems only in Irish – was Seán Ó Ríordáin, but I was blessed to have a number of brief meetings with him, nine times in fact. How do I know our meetings were exactly nine? Because in my teens, and later too, one of the books that captivated me was *Fíon na Filíochta*, the Irish poetry anthology I had studied in secondary school, most of which was sheer music to me. As a result, I felt forced to compose translations of many of the poems.

I was almost thirty when Ó Ríordáin's first collection was published. It completely bowled me over, because he was a modern, as impressive as the outstanding English poets I was then reading. He brought a new mental attitude to Irish poetry, but when he tried to explain it in his preface to his first collection, his explanation became involved in a reverberating controversy:

> What is poetry? The mind of a child? Imagine two in a room, a child and its father, and a horse passing along the street outside. The father looks out and says: 'That's Mr X's horse going to the Fair.' That is statement. By all appearances, the father loses the horse because he stays outside it. Call the horse a contagion. The father is not infected with the contagion. The horse does not enrich the father's life. But the child – he hears the sound of the horse. He tastes the sound of the horse for the sound's sake. And he listens to the sound getting less and less and falling down into silence. And the sound is a wonder to him and the silence is a wonder. And he considers the hind-feet of the horse and wonders at their authority and antiquity. And the world is full of horse-wonderment and trotting-spells. That is being. And that, to me, is poetry. The child lives in the guise of a horse …

That was the poet's explanation of poetry, and it was perfectly caught in the poem, 'Turnabout', which I could not refrain from translating.

> 'Come here,' said Turnbull, 'and see the sorrow
> In the horse's eyes,
> If you had his big hooves under you there'd be sorrow
> In your eyes too.'
>
> And 'twas clear that he well understood the sorrow
> In the horse's eyes.
> Had considered it until he had plumbed the very marrow
> Of the horse's mind.
>
> I gave a look at the horse to see the sorrow
> Standing up in his eyes,
> I saw Turnbull's eyes tracking me like an arrow
> From the horse's skull.
>
> I gave Turnbull a look that was mean and narrow
> And I saw in his head

Those over-big eyes that were dumb with sorrow –
The horse's eyes.

'Turnabout' was what brought me into contact with Seán Ó
Ríordáin, because I wanted to have my translation published somewhere, but I knew I would need his permission. So I went to Cork
City Hall where I ascertained he was working for Cork Corporation, and asked to see him. He saw me, he read my translation,
and to my relief and delight, he expressed his full satisfaction and
hoped it would be published. I sent it to *The Spectator* in London,
and it accepted it. That was the first of our nine meetings, for he
said he would like to see any further translations of his poetry and
I did eight more after 'Turnabout'.

Many of his critics of that day accused him of not being a native speaker. Ó Ríordáin was born in Ballyvourney, a then small
village in Co. Cork, his father being a native speaker although his
mother spoke only English. So English was the home-language,
but from the very beginning he was fluent too in Irish because
next door to him lived his old grandmother, a woman who had
only the language of her ancestors and who, pipe in fist, used to
recount to him night after night the ancient, wonderful, bardic
tales.

Much of the ground Ó Ríordáin's poetry covered was the same
ground T. S. Eliot's poetry covered: Sin, Repentance, the struggle
between Good and Evil in the soul. Sometimes, however, Ó Ríordáin's poetry sings with a despairing lyricism, as in 'The Invitation'.

I'd love to spend a night with thee,
To hear thy voice is sweet,
Thy lips are a divinity,
Thy sins a saint's defeat.

Oh, come to me and speak to me,
My thirst for thee is a goad;

Oh, dissipate the night with me,
Intoxicate my road.

Light up my looks – grow them an ear
For the coloured cry of the cows;
Draw near and I'll hear as clear as clear
The secret song of the rose.

My love, don't stay too far away
For this drunkenness fades like a smudge
And the river has only grammar to say
And I'm as dull as a judge.

Seán Ó Ríordáin, born in 1917, died in 1977. He was a truly
major poet.

Ancestral Voices

Priests are people, and in the nature of things more likely to be well-intentioned than not. I want to believe that. I need to believe it now. So does Ephraim.

I spent all my schooldays in St Dominick's, staffed almost exclusively by priests, and though their humours and reactions appeared to be the same as those of the few lay teachers, I still regarded them as a different species. When one of them stood in front of the class, book or pointer or chalk in hand, I did not see a man. I saw only a face above an all-enveloping black cassock that hid every line and sign of manhood. Ancestral voices had whispered that this creature was not as other men were, wouldn't think the thoughts other men thought, tell the jokes other men told, or want to kiss a girl. Ancestral voices warned that here was a living symbol of the apostasy that had riven the faith of my forefathers, Abraham, Isaac and Jacob, and in the process had taught the world to despise the Jews. And I took the warning to heart.

Ephraim was a few years older than me, and probably more mature too, and he didn't seem to be affected by much in the way of preconceptions or prejudices. He also went to St Dominick's, two classes ahead of me, but as we lived near each other we often walked home together when school ended. Ephraim was an only child, introspective, preoccupied, a lover of classical music, while I was a poetry lover, far more interested in books than in music.

Our homeward conversations were never of any consequence, due no doubt to our age gap, and the only brief, personal exchange we ever had was once when he asked me how I got on with my parents. I told him they were OK, and asked him how he got on with his. He merely snorted, as if he was recording his dissatisfaction, perhaps even annoyance.

When he finished his time at school and we were making our last walk home together, I complained that now I'd be stuck in St Dom's for another two years all by myself, since they had no other Jewish student.

'I suppose you'll be going to college,' I said.

'Oh yes,' he answered, with certainty and enthusiasm that I envied.

'And what are you going to do there?'

'Accountancy, I'm going to be an accountant. I love figures. They're like music. One figure follows another and the combination makes a melody.'

It was such an interesting idea, and an insight into the way his mind worked. He must have known for some time what he wanted to do with his life. Unfortunately, consideration about my own future had never before occurred to me. It didn't occur now either. With two more years in St Dom's still to go, my future seemed too far off to worry about. Summer had arrived, and I felt like a prisoner released. What, however, I didn't realise then was that although we may shape our own ends, we have little control over our beginnings, those feared preludes to experience.

It happened one summer afternoon that year. Early in the morning I had gone by train to Youghal, a seaside resort thirty miles from Cork, taking sandwiches, a flask of milk and a book. Sitting up on a hillock at the end of the long strand was the perfect spot to enjoy the sort of blissful, solitary withdrawal I rather wallowed in, and it being midweek and not a soul around, I spent hours lazing in the sun, daydreaming and reading. Later, as I sat in the deserted railway station waiting for the train back to the city, I was still happily sunk in my book.

'I think the train must be a bit late.'

Those were the first words Father Damien spoke.

I looked up, startled to hear a voice address me, and even more startled by the person it came from. Towering over me was this tall howitzer shape, all coal-coloured and dark with the sun inked out behind his black hat and the clerical collar almost hidden under a strong, shadowed chin.

'No,' I replied, timidly disagreeing, 'it's not due for a while.'

'Ah, that explains why it isn't even in the station yet. I thought for sure it'd be ready and waiting.'

This time I didn't reply – I was too involved in listening to my ancestral voices, until the priest cut in by inviting me to move up and make room for him, even though there was probably plenty of room on either side where I sat in the middle of the bench.

Of course I moved – priests weren't argued with or defied in those days, certainly not by the young, and least of all by a Jewish schoolboy. But this Jewish schoolboy had his ancestral voices to contend with, so in an effort to discourage further conversation I moved right to the extreme edge of the seat and buried my head back in my book. I see now how churlish my behaviour was; I can only hope that Father Damien put it down to shyness.

'Which one are you reading?' he asked as soon as he was seated.

I looked at him vacantly, noticing the soft blue eyes behind the heavy spectacles.

'Which one? Which poem?'

He had seen the name Yeats on the cover of my book. I made an involuntary move to put my hand over it but he pretended not to notice, easing my embarrassment by not waiting for an answer.

'Do you read a lot of poetry?'

I mumbled something that must have been unintelligible.

'Ah yes,' he replied, lifting his voice at the end to cut off my retreat.

Even now, recollection of that moment of panic makes me go cold. Never before had I felt so trapped. I had spent all my youth grazing inside my ancestral stockade, protected from any close contact with outsiders. Now here I was, fully exposed to one of those outsiders – and a priest moreover.

'I used to read a lot of poetry when I was your age,' he said half to himself. There was a sadness in his voice and he looked straight ahead as he spoke, almost as if he was looking back towards some lost paradise. I was lulled into a response.

'Did – did you read Yeats?'

'I did indeed. Do you know his poem "Sailing to Byzantium"? *An aged man is but a paltry thing, A tattered coat upon a stick, unless soul clap its hands and sing ...* That was my favourite. That line, *unless/Soul clap its hand and sing ...* It's such an exciting image. There's something mystical about it – the corporeal and the incorporeal all in one. Take a beautiful day like today: wouldn't it just make your soul clap its hands and sing?'

Hearing the priest praise that line increased my unease. I knew souls were important to Catholics, but I had never heard any talk of them at home. I didn't even know if I had one. And mixed in with my fear of the subject was embarrassment at my ignorance.

And at that moment it wasn't only my embarrassment at my ignorance that worried me. It was more, much more than that. The shock of meeting Father Damien and the sudden thought of two more years in St Dom's without Ephraim, had together visited on me my first cramping fear of the future I had never considered.

Immediately the train we had been waiting for arrived, a fat porter, his cap back on his head and a red handkerchief tied around his neck, scuttled to the exit to take the tickets from the few people who alighted. It was not a long train, and as the passengers disappeared there was hardly anybody left in it. I moved towards the third-class carriages in the rear, while Father Damien made to cross my path towards the first-class section. As I drew back and prepared to smile him away, he placed an arm around my shoulders and steered me along beside him.

'There's an empty carriage here,' he said.

It happened so unexpectedly, so swiftly, that I had no time to do anything about it. Docilely I stepped into the carriage, protesting that I didn't have a first-class ticket, but Father Damien directed me into a corner seat and settled himself back opposite me, saying, 'Sure that needn't worry you.' Then he leaned across and gave my knee a comforting squeeze.

The first half of the journey that followed must have been something of a nightmare to me. I could think of nothing except how I would explain to the ticket collector my presence in a first-class carriage when all I had was a third-class ticket. My memory presents a jumble of green fields, cows and cottages seen through the carriage window, interspersed by sleepy stations that the train barely disturbed in its halting passage. Of Father Damien's conversation at that stage, or my part in it, nothing remains.

But I needn't have worried. When the carriage door was opened and the collector appeared, calling 'Tickets please', the priest smoothly took mine from my reluctantly outstretched hand and gave it up with his. Even as the collector's eyebrows rose and his mouth opened to challenge me, Father Damien said quickly, 'That's all right – the boy's with me.' The reaction was instantaneous: a soft grunt of obeisance, an ingratiating smile, a touch of the cap – and the collector was gone.

I should have felt relief. I did, but only for a few moments, for soon Father Damien had started to chatter again.

'What parish are you from?' I hesitated, confused. 'I don't know. I mean I don't know its name.'

'Ah!'

His exclamation sounded self-satisfied, as if my answer had confirmed some suspicion in his mind.

He knows you're a Jew, the ancestral voices warned. *Be care-*

ful. But what was it I had to be careful of? No one had ever really explained.

'Where do you go to school?' he asked.

I told him. He nodded and commended the school's record.

'I suppose you'll be one of their Scholarship prospects?'

I blushed – it was the kind of flattery that forced a blush – but I was more annoyed than embarrassed. Left-handed compliments based on assumed racial aptitudes were just as unthinking as would have been left-handed sneers on assumed racial stigmas.

'Do you get on well with the boys in your class, you do?'

I said I did.

'I suppose you're friends with some of them. Special friends, I mean,' he added when I appeared uncomprehending.

'Not special.'

'Perhaps you prefer the girls,' he said with a crooked smile.

I reddened. 'I don't know any girls. Except my sister. And she's much older than me.'

He turned his head away and fell silent for a while. Then he began to talk again, drawing my attention to a copse of elm trees that the train was passing. They reminded him of the Abbey, the place where he lived with many other priests. He went on to tell me about it and about his life there. Detail by detail he built up a picture of warmth and peace and dedication. But there were moments when his voice trailed off, and in those silences he would look away from the window and turn his eyes on me. I felt uncomfortable under his soft stare, but took refuge in the knowledge that Cork and release were only a mile or two away.

He was still talking when the train reached its destination, and as he grew purposeful again, I found I was being assured how much I would like the abbey if I cared to visit it. Caught off guard, anxious only to escape, I nodded politely.

'Then how about next Tuesday? Can you manage that?'

Once again I was too slow, too taken by surprise, and my hesitation was sufficient to give him the wrong impression.

'Great,' he said as we stood outside the busy station, with the homegoing travellers hurrying past us. 'I'll pick you up here at seven-thirty on Tuesday.' Stooping a little to shake my hand, he murmured, almost confidentially, 'We can have more time together then,' before turning to disappear into the crowd.

I cursed my timidity, my reluctance to speak up for myself, and I determined that from there and then it was time for me to direct my own life. I wouldn't keep my appointment with Father Damien, I wouldn't spend another two years in St Dom's, I wouldn't go to college. I'd go to London, stay with my sister until I'd get a job, and make myself into someone I could recognise as a real person. And I would tell my parents my plan that evening.

I waited until they had finished their dinner, and unable to delay for another moment I revealed all my decisions.

After a silence, my father cleaned his spectacles and then addressed me.

'My son, what you have proposed doesn't make sense. On the other hand, it's not exactly non-sense. The best it makes is half sense, which is the best your father and mother could have expected from our son who is now only fourteen. I'm glad you are thinking about your future, and showing courage to tackle it. So I'll meet you halfway. If you finish your next years in St Dom's and pass your Leaving Certificate, I'll help you to go to London, and I'll keep you there for a reasonable length of time to get a reasonable job that will give you a start. If you fail to get a start, you will still have your Leaving Certificate, and so I would expect you to come back home, go to college, find what profession attracts you, and get the sort of qualifications that would give you a future. Remember, my son, on this night you have made it clear that you want to make your future your own way. Whether you succeed that way or not, we will still be proud of the son we love and who has never given us a moment of unhappiness. But, if you don't succeed your way, you'll still be so young that we'd want you to come back, as I suggest, and try to get a degree in something you would like and that would give you a fruitful and worthwhile life.'

My father was always an impressive logician and a great talker. I always believed that if he had had the opportunity, he could have been a solicitor, a barrister, or even a judge. At any rate, he and my mother were of one mind. I went first to my mother and kissed her, which was not unusual; I went then to my father and kissed him too, the only time I ever did.

That my parents showed their interest in my unexpected plans and their willingness to support me gave me the strength to stick to my very first intention – not to meet Father Damien on the following Tuesday.

The last two years in St Dom's were anything but dull, because as each month passed, I would be one day excited and next day anxious. I had to make absolutely certain that I would pass my Leaving Cert, not so much for myself as for my parents, who had given me the encouragement I needed. At the end everything went well, and when the day dawned for me to set off for London, I felt primed with enthusiasm and brimful of expectation.

I had thought I was prepared not to be bowled over by London, but that first sight of that metropolis was like being dumped on an unimaginable new world. Walking its streets made me feel as scared as a lost child. Lucky for me to be staying with my sister, for she was able to tell me that her very first experience of London was exactly the same as mine. Better still, how she had got over it quickly was by finding a job, any job, as soon as possible. Being employed, and soon having to pay tax too, helped her to regard herself as a semi-citizen. Which of course was exactly what I would have to become.

Well before I had left Cork I had come to the conclusion that working in a bookshop would be into my barrow, so I lost no time in noting down from the London telephone directory the names of all the bookshops in Hampstead, an area near where my sister lived. I tried them one by one, but on the first two days none of

them could take me on. On the very next day however, although
the first one I went to had no vacancy either, its very friendly
manager told me about another shop he thought might be willing
to try me, and I was to mention his name. I did, and it worked.
Eureka!

I phoned the news to my parents and of course they were
delighted, and very relieved. From then on my mother wrote to
me every fortnight, ostensibly to give me local and communal
news but mainly to get occasional replies from me. In fact both
hers and mine were rather heavy going – the Cork Jewish community was by then down to only a few hundred, so any news of
interest from it was sparse. Her single big surprise was that Ephraim had married. It astounded me – he was only twenty-one and
his wife was not from Cork, but from Leeds. They must have fallen in love, I thought, though I wondered how they had met. Fair
enough, and I sent him and her my congratulations. A year later
I had to repeat the dose on the birth of a daughter, Miriam, and
yet again another year's news of a further arrival, a son, Eddie, had
me back on my congratulatory trail. Eph's grateful reply asked me
how I was getting on. I told him that I often thought about our
companionship at St Dom's – which was somewhat of an exagge-
ration – and that I had been working in a bookshop but then got
a better and more interesting post in a medium-sized literary agency.

Very soon afterwards, however, my mother sent me a special
note that Eph's wife had died suddenly. Naturally it completely
shocked me, and it went through my mind that I might have
attended her burial if I could have got back to Cork for it in time.
All I could do instead was send him my heartfelt condolences. I
received from him a very brief letter of thanks, and I contem-
plated that such a tragedy would obviously change the course of
his life and might well mark the end of our correspondence.

To my amazement he wrote to me again one month later, a
long, philosophical, personal letter, the main message of which
was that he would concentrate on devoting his life to his children

and his work. He said, too, that he hoped I would keep writing to him and he promised not to fill his replies with too much boring family news. Naturally I was comforted by his description of me as a special friend.

The days, the months, the years passed, and by then one of my later letters commented that our epistolary exchanges were well consolidated by regarding ourselves as a pair of established penpals. His approbatory reply was that our age gap was now a *nihil*, having passed away as an adolescent mirage, and he half-jocularly – but, I had no doubt, with meaningful intent – wrote that I should get a wife for myself and raise a family. Look at mine, he said, recounting that Miriam had grown up so quickly, she now urged him to 'get with it', that he was 'antediluvian', while Eddie was a confident, athletic, normal boy – 'laid back' was what Eph used as if he had only recently learned the term. Very soon afterwards our relationship became even more important to me when my parents came over to live in London, having eventually accepted that by now I, as well as my sister, would definitely remain as permanent residents there. It meant that Ephraim was left as my only connection with Cork. When I passed the news on to him he replied by return post that it was time I paid Cork a visit, see how the city had changed in the twenty years since I had departed, he had a room waiting for me and he would love me to meet his children. Would I say yes, and if not, why not? Why not, I asked myself? Was it that I had always hidden in the back of my mind the recollection of the only person in Cork whose hand in friendship my forgotten ancestral voices had told me to reject – Father Damien?

I immediately accepted Eph's invitation.

I took an evening weekend flight, Eph collecting me at the airport and driving me to his home in a built up suburb that I could remember as once an empty country field. On the way he said that Miriam was an excellent cook and would have dinner ready for us.

'Lovely grub,' I laughed, 'lovely grub. I used to think it was a special Cork phrase. And you still have that noticeable touch of a Cork accent too.'

'Of course, I have,' he laughed back at me. 'Remember, I have a musical ear, and when you have a musical ear, you can't lose the accent you grew up with. You've lost it a bit yourself though, haven't you?'

'Probably. But I haven't gained a big beard like you have. I almost didn't recognise you when you came over to greet me.'

'Yes, it's such a relief when most of my work is done at home, which means I don't have to shave often. So it occurred to me that I might as well cut out shaving altogether. Hence the beard.'

To be with Eph again after so many years and letters had passed between us was probably what made us, during the longish drive from the airport, search for chit-chat to avoid embarrassing silences. When we were at St Dom's I really hardly knew him at all, nor he me, but now we had to know each other as real, talking friends, instead of correspondents, who could take time to think about what we wanted or needed to say. At least now that I was back in Cork, one thing I didn't have to worry about was what I would have to say to Father Damien. When he had told me on the train about the abbey where he lived, he hadn't mentioned its name, so there was no way I could reach him – even if he was still alive. I had fretted about it on the plane over, knowing that at moments in my life I was certain to be haunted by the way I had treated him. My only consolation was that I had very quickly learned never again to be straitjacketed into obeying the nonsensical authority of fabular ancestral voices. To banish them again and to keep the conversation going with Eph I told him how much I was looking forward to meeting Eddie.

'He won't be with us for dinner,' Eph answered. 'He's playing an important match tomorrow and he has a special tactics talk with his coach this evening. But he'll be back soon afterwards and you'll meet him then.'

'A match? Playing what?'

'Oh, forgive me. I probably never told you he's crazy-mad about rugby. He's St Dom's captain and leading player. Or so I'm told anyway. Unfortunately, I can't take to rugby. It's a very rough game, and sport shouldn't be rough. To call rugby a sport is really a contradiction in terms.' Eph sighed before adding, 'But he's my son. I couldn't possibly stop him playing, and to be truthful, I'm proud that he excels at it. At least he's always avoided any serious injury, the odd bruise but nothing else. Now, here we are, the old homestead.'

Miriam was there to greet me and she didn't wait to be introduced.

'You're very welcome. Dad so often talks about you, and you look exactly like what I expected.'

'Thank you, Miriam. And I can tell you that you, too, are exactly like the young lady he's often mentioned in his letters.'

'I hope he has,' she laughed, and winking at Eph, added, 'I'd brain you if you hadn't, Dad.'

In fact she was just as he had described, attractive, stylish, and as Eph had labelled her in one of his letters, 'with it'. When, I wondered, were sixteen-year-olds young nowadays?

It was after dinner when Eddie arrived, with a young-looking man.

'Dad, this is my coach, Pat,' he said. 'I made him come in with me so you could meet him. I thought it was time you should know each other.'

Eph shook the unexpected visitor's hand and welcomed him, then he introduced me to Eddie, and then, describing me as his schoolfriend from the days we had both been together at St Dom's, he introduced Eddie's coach to me as Father Pat. The 'mod' get-up completely threw me. He was wearing a t-shirt and jeans. Indeed, if it hadn't been for his slightly advancing baldness I could almost have taken him and Eddie to be classmates! I don't think I'd have been too ill-at-ease if he had been dressed like a normal priest, though paradoxically it had been the opposite when I was confronted with Father Damien. In *his* case it was the sight of the collar and black cloth that alarmed me – that and the quiet smile so full of presumption. When I shook hands with Eddie's coach, I stumbled over calling him 'Father'. I couldn't take in hearing Eddie calling him Pat. Miriam was of course also introduced, calling out a breezy 'Hi', and the priest echoed it back, raising a brisk, open-handed salute, Red Indian-style. Eph fetched us three beers – Eddie and Miriam had soft drinks – and we all chatted sociably.

That was the first conversation of any length I had had with a priest since my meeting with Father Damien. But what a difference between the two encounters! With Pat I was Eph's guest, which put me in the position of having to be friendly; with Father Damien I had been intent on keeping myself to myself.

When talking to Father Pat about rugby I was embarrassed by my ignorance of the game. Eph, too, said little about it, keeping off his criticism of the sport. When Father Pat put his arm around Eddie's neck in a comradely hug, saying, 'This young man will be a star one day. Take it from me – he'll play for Ireland yet,' Eddie blushed at the compliment and slapped his coach's hand in mock chastisement.

'Wouldn't you both come along tomorrow and see him play?' Father Pat suggested. 'You could come with Eddie. Or if that's too early for you, ask for me at the gate when you arrive and I'll collect you. You'll get the best seat in the park – right next to me on the coach's bench.'

'That's very good of you,' I smiled, but Eph said nothing as if my smile included his. But knowing Eph's feelings I didn't expect we'd be accepting Father Pat's offer. I nearly caused the same misunderstanding with Father Pat's as I had with Father Damien's offer when I didn't immediately decline the former's invitation to the match. Fortunately, however, this time I was given a second chance. As he was being left to the door by Eddie, Eph and me, he said, 'I'll see you tomorrow, will I?' and I was able to reply, 'I'll do my best. But don't rely on it.'

'What did you think of him?' Miriam asked after Eph and I had seen him and Eddie to the door for their already arranged brisk training walk.

'He seems all right,' I said. 'A nice enough man. Not what I'd have expected a priest to look like. But then these days …'

'He's as queer as a coot, of course,' Miriam said, quite conversationally.

'Queer? How do you mean?' Eph asked her.

She looked at him, a pained expression on her face.

'Oh, daddy! Where *have* you been all these years! He's gay – as gay as they come. Surely you must have noticed.'

I looked at Miriam with some amazement. I hadn't noticed. I never do notice these things. They had never been part of the world I had engaged in. Discos, drugs, sex, gays – they were the world of Miriam's generation.

'Are you sure?' I asked.

'Of course I'm sure. A blind man could see it.'

'No, my daughter,' Ephraim exclaimed angrily. 'A blind man couldn't see it. A blind man sees nothing. Like your father. What else hadn't I seen?'

Suddenly it hit me and my heart lurched. If Father Pat was gay, was Eddie too? And was that what Eph was thinking also? Was it what had made him so angry?

If I had the chance I could have asked Miriam, she was so knowing. But now would I believe her if she told me he wasn't? Homosexuality probably didn't upset her, but she could have no doubt about the effect it would have on Eph if he knew that his son … I began to think about the friendship between Eddie and Father Pat – a Catholic priest and a Jewish youth. I began to read the worst about the way Father Pat had put an arm around Eddie's shoulders, and the embarrassed, almost dainty slap Eddie had given him. I was appalled. Could it possibly be? And was all this now torturing Eph? The newspapers were full of talk about homosexuality. More and more people were admitting openly to it. And priests were people too.

Then they started – the ancestral voices. After all those years they had come to life again and brought back what I had buried twenty years before: the memory of Father Damien. Chilling and stark, it bloomed in my mind, as if the rubble of the years between had merely served to keep it fresh and intact until something should happen to uncover it. Once more I was back in that carriage, feeling the grip of his hand on my knee, the hunger of his eyes on my face. Had he, too, been ...?

I told myself that even if Miriam had been right about Father Pat, that was no reason for me or Eph to suspect Eddie. We had nothing to go on. So Eddie had a friendship with a priest – so what? Just as so long ago I had had no convincing reason whatever to reject Father Damien. If I hadn't listened to those accursed ancestral voices, I, too, might well have had a normal friendship with him.

I was heartbroken too at the possibility of Eph having to question Eddie. Surely that sort of father and son man-to-man talk was hopelessly out-of-date. Boys nowadays learned everything about sex very early – how could they not? It was all around them.

At last Eph made a decision. Clearly he knew he had his duty to do, but he also knew he couldn't take the risk of questioning Eddie and then finding he was wrong. That would forever wreck his relationship with his son. So he decided to ask Miriam first, and ask her now.

She's a cool one, that girl. I thought the question would shock her, at the very least surprise her. But she took it in her stride. Hardly glancing up from her magazine, she shrugged her shoulders and said, 'I don't know. It never struck me. I never thought about it.'

'Do you mean,' Eph pursued hesitantly, 'that it never struck you Eddie might be ...? Or that you never thought about it at all?'

'Never thought about it at all really.'

'Think about it now, Miriam,' Eph coolly insisted.

She put her magazine aside and thought about it. For a whole second. Then she gave her verdict. 'I mean, we don't see a good deal of Eddie, do we, so it's hard to tell. Besides, when you live with someone, you don't notice some things. Same with your friends. I mean, ten per cent of the male population is supposed to be gay, so how many of your friends are, without you knowing? You could be one of the ten per cent yourself and *they* needn't know, need they?'

'Miriam!'

She laughed. 'Joke, dad, only a joke.'

She said no more. It was obvious that she couldn't, or wouldn't help her father. Something told me too that she would make sure of getting to Eddie before Eph could. How ironic! With Father Damien it was ancestral voices that had kept me in ignorance, and now Eph's own children might well be doing the same.

Is there a lesson for us somewhere in all this?

A Long Walk from the Past, a Short Walk to the Future

I was thinking that Aaron was thinking it was time he went to bed. To sleep? Well yes, of course to sleep. But I could see in my mind that he was wondering what chance he had of getting a wink of sleep after his own foolishness. What in the world had made him say to Catherine, 'Tomorrow's journey will be a pleasant trip to the Marina.' Why, how, did such an idea come to him? Certainly, weather permitting, they could get out of the car and walk – not merely walk, just rove, airborne, along the straight, smooth Marina under the arched trees, benches dotted along the path, and the mowed grass bank sloping down to the flowing Lee voyaging alongside its Tivoli vista. And hadn't he also said that he had 'a special reason for wanting to go there, two special reasons in fact to tell you about'. Two special reasons? What could they be? How could I have put them in Aaron's mind when I had no idea what they were? There was absolutely no connection between the Marina and Cork's Jewish community. So was there something else, something exceptional, that he knew and I didn't?

Suddenly I remembered who it was, at the beginning of this book, had inspired me to undertake the seemingly absurd pursuit of tracing, unearthing, unravelling, thus somehow discovering sufficient material to fill this second volume of autobiography – it was Marcel Proust, who had taken 'as the starting-point, in his discovery of time past and gone, his moments of involuntary memory'. Well and good, I thought, but only up to a point, for Proust's idea was only halfway to my starting-point for detecting what was in Aaron's mind. The lift-off was the echo of a starting-gun that had been exploded by a living writer less than two years older than I, Norman Mailer. He wrote in a recent essay 'In the course of fashioning a character, you invariably reach a point where you recognise that you don't know enough about the person you are trying to create. At such times, I take it for granted that my unconscious knows more than I do ... To use an unhappy analogy, the unconscious is a powerful computer that rarely needs new sources to fashion a portrait, because so much knowledge has already been stored away.'

How bang-on Mailer was. Immediately I put Aaron and Catherine into her car and sent them off on the approach road to the Marina, and Aaron without any delay gave tongue.

'For me this isn't the real Marina, Catherine, not until we get to the unblemished, unexploited part that brings the river Lee into full view. What we're passing now wasn't the threshold of the wonder-world Marina that meant so much to me when I was a youth. This, here, is the later, modern Industrial Estate that took over the originally uninhabited and unbuilt-upon land where Henry Ford established his motor factory in 1917. But look at it now, a crushing factory-city that has blotted out nature. It's painful to look at it. At least when Ford's was put there, all by itself, it was something worth going to see and wonder at. Even when Dunlop's, the famous tyre makers, went up next door, there was still acres of space and view for nature to thrive around it. Not now there isn't. Ford's and Dunlop's are a long time gone, and what's taken its place is a mass of anything and everything but space and air. I suppose you've seen all this before, Catherine?'

'Well, not properly. I've hardly ever come down here and I never bothered to look around me. I suppose I should feel ashamed, shouldn't I?'

'Ah, not really, my dear, not really,' Aaron allowed. 'You're a new generation, a new city-generation that has to live where its grandparents and antecedents had streets and fields to roam in and they could stretch their legs and stop to stare without being tripped up by people rushing around. Ah, but don't mind me giving out, Catherine. I'm an old fogey who has outlived his time. Anyway, it's great to have at least you I can spout at and who won't complain.'

Catherine squeezed his hand and laughed.

'Spout away, Aaron, I love listening to you and learning about the Cork I didn't know. And you're the youngest "old fogey" I've ever met. So there. Now tell me, was Henry Ford one of the reasons you've brought me out here? I know virtually nothing about him except that he started the Ford car.'

'Yes, he certainly did that. And the Ford car is still going strong.'

'Was he born in Cork?'

'No, he wasn't born in the city of Cork. He came from a village known as Ballinascarty, thirty miles west of Cork. I suppose few know or remember that now. Indeed, I have one of those massive British biographical dictionaries that says he was born in the US. Ignoramuses!' Aaron exclaimed.

Catherine stopped the car, sensing that Aaron's desire to tell her about Henry Ford might well be one of the two special reasons he had for this visit to the Marina.

'Well, my girl, I must admit I have mixed feelings about the great Henry Ford. He was, when he was alive, a very charismatic man – it's fair to say he was a legend in his time. Indeed, really brilliant people often become legends in their time because comments or sayings are often ascribed to them, though one is never sure the famous words were their own. The still-remembered wisecrack Ford is supposed to have made about the first cars he built is "You can have any colour car you want, as long as it's black". And for a fairly long time all cars were indeed black.'

'Sounds like there was a touch of humour in him,' Catherine laughed.

'If not in him, then about him. There was another one too. When I was a youngster there was a verse about Henry Ford that everyone in Cork knew. It went like this:

There once was a man whose name was Henry Ford.
He got a piece of rubber and a big piece of board.
He bought a pint of petrol in an old tin can,
And he put them all together and the damn thing ran.

'I've never forgotten that.'

'Oh that's a marvellous story, I must really use it in the paper,' Catherine declared as she made a note of the verse.

'Yes, I thought it might appeal to you.'

'Any more about him, Aaron,' she asked.

'Yes, there is more, but I'm not sure I should tell you,' Aaron said quietly.

'Why ever not? Was he a womaniser? Is that it?'

'Not that I know of,' Aaron admitted. 'But what I do know is something I don't think is known about him in his own country. And the people, especially in Cork, mightn't like to learn it ...'

'Well, tell me anyway. I'll use my own judgement, you can rely on that.'

Aaron paused a while before shaking his head slowly from side to side. Then, 'I'm sorry to have to say that Henry Ford was a known anti-Semite. It was in the US he made his comments. I read about it years ago in a biography or perhaps even in a magazine article – unfortunately I don't remember where. Myself, I have mixed feelings. I always greatly admired his genius and achievement until I read what I read. It was a sorrowful blow to me, a Jew and a Corkman. Maybe if he had lived in Cork, preferably in or near Jewtown, he'd have learned what was good about the Jews. Now, Catherine, let's forget about Henry Ford and drive on to the real Marina. As I told you, it's very special to me.'

'OK Aaron, here goes to what sounds like your paradise. Do you want to stop somewhere or shall we keep going till it ends?'

'Every paradise ends, on this earth anyway. So stop at the beginning, we'll take a brief walk, and then sit ourselves on a bench and talk.'

As their walk commenced, Aaron held Catherine's arm.

'The Marina is quite a long walk – about halfway there's a bend in the road, so until you reach it, you don't realise that there's a fair bit more you have to go to get to the end. But the distance doesn't greatly worry because there's so much to see. Soon enough ahead of us there was a small, two-sided, sheltered shed. Did you ever sit in it, Catherine?'

'I saw it many years ago, but I don't remember ever having sat in it.'

'Ah, well if you did, I'm sure you wouldn't have forgotten that.'

'Why?' Catherine asked.

'Because it's a place where young men and their girls often cuddled.'

A pause before Aaron commented, 'I suppose you're wondering if I used to cuddle there.'

Catherine laughed. 'Well, did you?'

He didn't respond to her enquiry.

'Let's sit here for a while, look at the river and admire the view. Right across the Lee, on the other side is Tivoli, a really attractive scene I'm sure you must know of. But do you know that many years ago there was a regular ferry service from there when there was a match in the Athletic Grounds a bit ahead and behind us, and all the hurling fans from Tivoli and that side took the ferry across? And another interesting thing – though it, too, is long gone – was a cannon, very near the covered shed. It was a relic of the Crimean War and, believe it or not, it used to be fired once every day to mark Greenwich Mean Time.

'Then in the summer there was a lot of rowing on the Lee,

famous races organised by the Lee and Shandon Boat Clubs. The Leander Cup races drew teams from all over Europe. Oh, these were the times of a very different, very civilised world. And the river gets wider as it flows along all the way into Lough Mahon, passing Blackrock Castle at the end of the Marina. Everything about the Marina tells you why I once loved it – at least it's why I told you about it, Catherine, because it's the Marina of the past now. And that brings me to the second reason I wanted us to come here together. You asked me if I used to cuddle in that shed. Well, my dear, that's the real story of my life, and I want to tell it to you now. For your own ears only.'

'Of course, of course. You can trust me.'

'I know, Catherine, I know. If I didn't know I can trust you, I'd not be opening my mouth. I'd die silent.'

'Look, Aaron,' said Catherine, 'let's go back to your place where you'll be so much more comfortable. I'll get food on the way, rustle up a nice lunch, and after it you can sit yourself back.'

'You're so right, my girl, you think of everything. But I won't have you paying for the food.' He put some money in her hand.

'You think of everything too,' she said, smiling.

After lunch Catherine washed up, and then together they made themselves comfortable. Aaron relaxed for a moment and then commenced.

'I've already told you a little about my parents and their death of the flu in London when I was six. I told you they had asked Misha and his wife to take care of me while they were away, and when they died, Misha said that I would continue to live as one of his family. I never knew or understood why they had gone to London – as you'll recall, I just wondered whether my mother had been pregnant, or perhaps she hadn't been pregnant, but wanting to have another child she found she just couldn't, and was told London was the place where she'd find a well-known maternity hospital that would advise her. As you'll have seen, Catherine, I

was in such total ignorance about them that as I grew up I kept
working out ridiculous ideas as possible answers for their journey.

'Anyway, soon Misha made me his apprentice in his tailoring
business, and I began to learn about it all in very quick time. In
fact, I became an expert myself. And then came the beginning to
the rest of my life – the second beginning, the real story.

'At that time, the youngsters, the Jewish boys and girls of
Jewtown, formed a social club. They met in a small hall in Marlborough Street and used hold short Saturday night dances, but
once a month the dance was an all-night one. And I do mean all-
night. It would start at eight o'clock and finish at six in the morning. There'd be tea, cakes and sandwiches served not just once,
but a second time at about three or four in the morning. The tickets cost half-a-crown – that's two shillings and sixpence in old
money – and we sold tickets to many Catholic friends. One of
them would be our MC, master of ceremonies, who'd get a com-
plimentary ticket for himself and one for his girlfriend. And all
wore evening dress. Yes, believe it or not, evening dress. And
what's more, everyone received a printed programme with pencil
supplied. What do you think of that?'

Catherine's mouth was wide open with surprise.

'It's wonderful, almost unbelievable. And open to non-Jews
too. It just shows you the ties between the Jews and Catholics of
Jewtown. The more I learn from you about Jewtown, the more I
wouldn't have minded living there in those days.'

Aaron chuckled. 'If you had,' he said, 'we'd certainly have
met. Everyone knew each other because it was considered our
duty to welcome any non-Jewish boys or girls we didn't already
know. And when the dance ended at six o'clock sharp on Sunday
morning, we'd all walk together, the Jews going to their homes,
and when the Catholics came to a church, they'd say goodbye to
us and go into the church for Sunday mass.'

'Incredible,' Catherine declared, 'and so beautiful. What a
story that would make for my feature. Would it be all right for me

to use that bit, Aaron? Only if you agree, of course.'

'Yes, by all means use that. But what follows is what you might call my secret-life – and now your secret too. At one of those dances I met a Catholic girl, we got on great, liked each other, and when she came again to our next all-night dance, we spent a lot of time together, just dancing, talking. I – foolishly, I suppose – asked her if she'd come out for a walk with me some night. She said she'd love to. And that was the beginning.

'I wasn't in love with her – certainly not then anyway, even if I ever was. But what I did fall in love with then was the Marina. It was where we went on our walks, about two evenings every week for the next couple of months. We used meet there because it was convenient for both of us – she didn't live in Jewtown but not far from it – and also of course we wanted to avoid being seen together. Our meeting place was the covered shed, and because many times there'd be no one else sitting on the bench that faced the river, we couldn't be seen by people passing on the path. With the river before us we also had the view of Tivoli on the other side, and if it wasn't too dark an evening, we could see down the full stretch of the Lee to Blackrock Castle. That was the first time I kissed a girl – Una was her name – we just kissed and cuddled, that was all. Nothing else was ever in my head, and I'm sure it wasn't in Una's either, we were just little more than youngsters. We liked each other a great deal, and we both fell in love with the Marina. I suppose our enjoyment of each other would have been a factor in our love of the place. After all, it was special be-cause there was no other place we could go.

'You couldn't say we were sweethearts. We never had any of that sort of talk. Who knows, if we had been together for more than a few months ... but there's no point in thinking about that. Our friendship – that's what I'd call it now – lasted only those few months before the blow came. Someone from the Jewish commu-nity saw us – it must have been on some evening when we had to sit on one of the ordinary benches on the river bank – I never found out who it was, and it made no difference to me who it might have been because he told Misha.'

'Oh my God!' Catherine exclaimed. 'That's awful.'

'Well, really it might have been the best thing for us. It certainly taught us something about life, and anyway, if we had gone on to really fall in love, we would have been faced with a much bigger problem.

'I saw Una on one more evening – we always had to pre-arrange our next meeting – and I told her what had happened and that we couldn't meet again. She took it very well. She didn't get annoyed or distressed or cry. She said she understood. She thanked me for liking her ...'

Aaron couldn't continue immediately and Catherine saw how upset he was. She thought perhaps his recollection of Una thanking him for liking her was almost too much for him to bear. After a pause, he resumed.

'When we parted, she kissed me goodbye. Pecked me would be more like it. She was such an understanding girl. She knew that under the circumstances an embrace wouldn't help either of us feel any better.'

Quietly Catherine said, 'I suppose it was Misha who insisted you stop seeing Una.'

'Yes, it was Misha. But I could hardly blame him. I remember everything he said. He was reasonable – and surprising too. He said that if I kept seeing the girl – that's what he called her because he didn't know her name – if I kept seeing her I would bring shame on the community as well as on his wife and himself, along with the great sorrow they would feel. "You have lived with us for over ten years," he said, "and we have treated you as our son and we regard you as our son. But if you decide to continue as you're doing now, you could no longer be a son of ours. You would have to leave and try to find a home elsewhere." Misha stopped for a moment, as if thinking over what he'd said, and I felt he had more to say, so I held my tongue.

'Then he went on to tell me that if I gave him my word to forget about what I had done, he would forget it too, and "You'd be our son, Aaron, again, What's more," he added, and this has never left my mind in all the years that have passed, because it started a whole traumatic enigma for me. "What's more, my business would pass on to you – the girls want to go to college, not into the business – and if my business should do well, as I believe it will, I would make my will to benefit all my family. I must repeat, *all* my family." And he finished with one more offer, that if I continued to be his apprentice, he would increase my weekly wage.

'Well, what alternative was there? I knew immediately that I had to give up going with Una. I wasn't in love with her – if I stayed with her perhaps love would grow, but what could I have done about it? Marry her? Out of the question. And maybe she wouldn't have wanted to marry me anyway. So, as I've told you, we said goodbye.'

'And what about Misha?' Catherine queried. 'Did you stay with him?'

'Of course. Again, what alternative did I have to what he offered me? None, of course. Yet what soon was far more important to me was the way my mind became obsessed with my old question. What was so surprising was Misha's generosity. Surely, I thought, he didn't need to be as generous as he'd been, for he knew I couldn't possibly hold out against him. But it wasn't what he said. What obsessed me was the way he said it, the particular words he used. He kept on referring to me as his son, that his will would benefit all his family, and he repeated "all my family", especially emphasising "all". But once, just only once, he said, "You'd be our son, Aaron, again." Had he meant to use my name as his son, or was it an accidental slip of his tongue that revealed me to be his and his wife's true child?'

'I can see why that brought back to you all over again the dilemma of why your parents went to London,' said Catherine.

'Yes, only worse than before. If I wasn't their child, is it really

possible that Misha and his wife agreed to give me to them because no matter how hard they had tried to have a child, they
were heartbroken that they always failed, or maybe they even did
have a child, perhaps more than one, but it was always stillborn.
After all, Misha and his wife must have been their closest friends
who already had two growing-up children, and may have found a
third child too big a financial burden for them at that time, so as
a blessing to their best, childless friends, they gave me to them.
Remember, Misha told me that when my parents died in London,
he hadn't the money to bring them back and be buried in Cork.
The whole conundrum drove me mad, Catherine, all those crazy
ideas. It went on for months. Sometimes I felt like killing myself.'

'Oh no, Aaron, no. Not that.'

'Well, I did. But things changed, changed suddenly and so
amazingly that I just couldn't credit what happened. The first time
I went to our Saturday night dances after the terrible worries I
had gone through, I met a girl. A Jewish girl, from Leeds, who had
never been in Ireland before. She was pretty, intelligent, and a
good talker, a straightforward talker. She was staying with friends
of her parents, and I saw her, well, virtually every night of her
stay. I began to like her more and more, and I thought she liked
me too. I thought that was why she had told me the reason she
had come to Cork.

'Her name was Leah. None of the local Jewish girls had that
name, though I had read it in the Bible, in Genesis. Jacob's wife
was called Leah and she became one of the four matriarchs of the
Jewish people. Well, my Leah was a sort of matriarch too, because
she was honest and tough. Very honest and very tough – even
though she was only about a year younger than me. Her story was
that her father was very wealthy and wanted her to go to university in Leeds. She didn't want to go to university. She wanted to
go into business, but not with her father. She wanted to marry
early and raise a family as soon as she could find a good husband
she could love. She felt no attraction for any of the Jewish boys

in Leeds, and she said that some had been after her because they knew she had inherited a lot of money from her dead grandfather.

'Leah made quick and firm decisions. She admitted that she had come to Cork to see if there were any of the Jewish boys there who might attract her, who liked her, and most of all, would be the kind of man who would suit her if they were to consider making a match.

'"Now," she said, "I've told you, truthfully, about myself. If you are interested, but only if you are really interested, tell me about your own life. I'd have to know all about you first, Aaron." What a matriarch type she certainly was, Catherine.'

'And you told her?'

'Yes, everything. About my parents, about Misha and his wife, about my parents' deaths – oh everything as I told you. About Una and parting from her when Misha found out and what he had said to me. The lot. Leah thought over it for a while and then asked what I was doing and what plans I had. I told her I was Misha's tailoring apprentice and that as soon as I could save up every penny, I'd start my own business as a tailor.

'She thought for a while again, and then she asked me if I might like her enough to marry her. I felt poleaxed by that. She had a great laugh at me herself and it amused me too. As a matter of fact, I think her laughter, and the reason for it, was what made me warm to her instead of just liking her. And I said so. So she said she'd stay here for another few weeks, we could be seeing each other and really getting to know each other, and then decide if we both felt happy about marrying. We couldn't expect to be in love with each other so quickly, but she had a true feeling that, as far as she was concerned, her love for me would soon grow. You know, Catherine, although she was younger than me, she was a far more mature and independent person. She sort of woke me. I think I should say she made me grow up.'

'And did you get married?'

'Oh yes, we did get married. But not, alas, for long.'

'What happened Aaron? Can you tell me, or would you prefer not to say any more? I'm sure it can't be easy.'

'Well, it was so long ago that it almost never enters my mind now. What happened was that we agreed to get married, and she decided to go to her parents and tell them about me. She told me that beforehand she would make her will to leave everything to me. She was going by plane because although she had feared coming over to Ireland by plane, she feared coming or going by water even worse.

'I'm afraid her father and mother were mad angry about marrying a nobody. That, of course, made Leah even more angry than them, so she just gathered all her clothes, flew straight back to Dublin, took the train to Cork – there was no plane to Cork then – took a taxi to where she was staying, and within two weeks we married. We had no wedding celebration because she suggested we should buy a house immediately, I should set up tailoring, she would join me in it, and we would belong to it together even though everything was paid by her. She told me exactly what she was worth – it was a very great deal of money indeed – and with my knowledge of tailoring, we both would have a successful and wonderful life. The only thing that worried her was the break-up with her parents. They wouldn't even answer her letters. So, a little after a year later, when all was going smooth with us, and our love for each other had grown, she became pregnant. We were both overjoyed by that, but she decided to fly back to her parents and beg them to be reconciled with her and come to visit and stay with us when our baby was born. She wrote to them, I left her at the station, and I never heard from her or saw her again. The plane crashed on landing. Leah and other passengers were killed. Her parents must have collected her body because they wrote to tell me that they had buried her in Leeds.'

Aaron said no more.

Catherine put her hand on his, her eyes moist with tears.

'Ah, Catherine. It's all over. I did my crying a long time ago.'

My Story Page Chase

When I retired from the *Irish Press* at the end of 1986, the person engaged to take over as editor of the weekly 'New Irish Writing' page from the beginning of 1987 was a writer whose first stories I had published in the page. He was Anthony Glavin, born in 1946, an Irish-American who had been living in Ireland for many years. However, his appointment ended in April 1988 simply because the broadsheet *Irish Press* became a tabloid and the short story page was abandoned. Unexpectedly, after not too long an absence, 'New Irish Writing' was rescued by the *Sunday Tribune*, edited at that time by Vincent Browne, and resuscitated in its popular form as a weekly full page. Unfortunately however, the highly promising restart period ended when the *Sunday Tribune* suddenly dropped the feature – only to bring it back after a silence of some months. But – yes, there was a 'but' to its return – the page would now appear only once each month. Then in due course the *Sunday Tribune* included with its newspaper a tabloid magazine – as indeed was by then the fashion of so many broadsheet newspapers – and it was into the restricted space of a once monthly tabloid page that 'New Irish Writing' was relegated.

By that time some two years had passed since I had left the *Irish Press*, and I began to notice that the short story biting bug had returned to infect me. What had brought it back? Firstly, it was the realisation that my old packhorse self was badly missing its weekly load of story manuscripts; secondly, although I was very glad that even in its truncated form in the *Sunday Tribune*, 'New Irish Writing' continued, along with the prestigious annual Hennessy Literary Awards, nevertheless, just twelve pages a year and the story length limited to some three thousand words in a tabloid page, seemed to me unlikely to be able to maintain the constant arrival of distinguished new Irish short story writers as the seventies and eighties had. Not that the foregoing is at all meant as a criticism of the *Sunday Tribune*. Its 'New Irish Writing' page has kept its own flag flying for years, and that's a real achievement.

So how did I try to get back into the short story's line of fire? My target, of course, was to persuade some leading broadsheet to take on a weekly story page, but over a number of subsequent years I learned that all my attempts were merely firing blank shots.

My first shot had to be strategically aimed, because it would be foolish, I thought, to choose an already in-the-field Dublin newspaper as my target. So my choice – in a sense it chose me – was the *Cork Examiner*, as it then was. It had a large circulation, covered Ireland's biggest province, and Cork was my home ground. I wrote to the managing director, briefly detailed my idea, and asked for his kind consideration.

Months passed. No answer. I wrote again. Same answer, i.e., total silence, not even an acknowledgement.

It was time for me to load up again, and my surprise target was not an Irish newspaper. It was the *Sunday Times*, which had recently opened an editorial office in Dublin. I decided to beard the Irish editor in his den without phoning or writing for an appointment, his office being directly opposite Government Buildings. He saw me without delay, was very cordial and listened to my suggestion that the *Sunday Times* might consider having a weekly Irish short story page. He found it an interesting idea, but could give it no thought at that moment because the paper was hoping to set up a printing plant of its own near Dublin, and everything depended on that. If I would let some months pass and then get in touch with him again, he would let me know the situation. I waited, I let the months pass, and I dropped in on him again. He expressed his regrets, the printing plant would not be set up, and that was that.

Having started, I wasn't going to give in yet, but I had to think of a rather different target that would need a bigger gun, and a bigger bullet too. And quite unexpectedly I had already been given the opportunity of finding my next target's range.

Out of the blue I had been invited by Waterstone's to launch their Cork bookshop. Such an invitation rather tickled me. I had no reason even to imagine that I would ever produce a new book that might be launched in Cork's Waterstone's, but to be chosen to launch its big, new premises was more than adequate substitute. Naturally I was introduced to whichever top brass came over from London for the event – was it the managing director himself perhaps? – and immediately I knew that Waterstone's would be my target, and my new missile would be a first-in-the-field idea.

The idea was the sponsorship of an annual International Short Story Award. At the time I was, myself, absolutely up in the air about it, but remembering it now, I am not only ashamed of such a nonsensical idea, but also amused that it was simultaneously both up in the air and off the wall. Before I came to my senses I wrote to the MD of Waterstone's, putting to him the idea of the International Short Story Award, and setting out the details of its proposed construction, administration, advantages for the sponsor, and anything else I could think of. Thank goodness I never got a reply. I can only hope now that whoever read the letter has long forgotten it – or is fortunate if in any moments of depression he is able to remember it for a good laugh.

Was that the end of my road? I remembered Samuel Beckett's advice that if you fail in anything, fail better next time, and suddenly I recalled the strange birth of the 'New Irish Writing' page. One morning I was making an off the cuff journey to the *Irish Times* to put to them my suggestion that they publish a weekly

short story. By chance my journey was diverted to the *Irish Press*
so as to put my idea to its editor, Tim Pat Coogan. I did so, and
the day's journey ended with the *Irish Press* becoming 'New Irish
Writing''s different hoped-for childbed. As it was the *Irish Times*
that had been my very first intended hope, and as I so much
wanted to revive a weekly short story page over twenty years after
I had founded it, why not return now to my original target?

The year was 1990, there was no time to lose, but I'd have no
more recourse to gun-and-bullet metaphorical weapons, not with
the *Irish Times*. For them I'd send out a respectful, graceful-look-
ing boomerang. I made my first throw of it to its then editor,
Conor Brady, on the first day of December, 1990. Its flight, and its
editor's replies, continued until 18 December 1998, comprising ten
letters from me and nine from Conor Brady.

Conor Brady's constant reservation about a weekly short story
page was in the main the paper's pressure on space. Nevertheless,
his replies were always speedy and sympathetic, and whenever I
thought up some possible new ways of getting around the space
difficulty, he usually passed on my ideas to the relevant department managers for their response. Nothing really hopeful ever
resulted from my letters – apart from the occasions when the *Irish
Times* was considering launching a Sunday paper which unfortunately didn't materialise – and then when expansion of the paper's
existing sections 'would restrict the development of entirely new
additions such as the weekly short story' our correspondence was
brought to its end. I never met Conor Brady, but the memory of
his unfailing diligence and graciousness has always stayed in my
mind.

As it happens, my exchanges with the *Irish Times* turned out
to be but my penultimate effort to find a home for a weekly short
story page. In the spring of 2002, I was able to have a meeting
with the Arts Council's Literature Officer who listened to my suggestion and expressed real interest in it. However, it was pointed
out that the Arts Council could not select just one particular

broadsheet paper to approach with my idea, they would have to write to every such paper in the country. Also, the board would first have to consider all the details and any possible grant involved. Consequently, no report could be expected before the following autumn.

When autumn went by without a report, I wrote and phoned the Arts Council and was told that the matter was getting their attention. That was the last I heard. So, clearly I had failed Samuel Beckett's advice.

My Cork Still Floats

Thirteen years is a long time for anyone to have been away from home. And as my home happened to be Cork, my birthplace, my departing farewell happened to be accompanied by my co-travelling excess baggage of memories that would eventually begin to deliver its charge.

My destination was London, but my real destination was a hoped-for future as an established writer. London, surely, was where it was all happening, where it would happen for me. It didn't, and that wasn't London's fault; it was my own, for two reasons. The first one was too much youthful inexperience. The second reason – the major one – was that I had grown too big for my roots. If a writer grows too big for his roots, in all probability he just dries up. Within two years of my arrival in London, the miraculous little unseen bottle of ink that every writer carries inside him and which must flow through all his blood vessels, disappeared into thin air. It happened gradually, slowly – but not so slowly that I didn't feel it happening. My hoped-for future as a writer had faded away because I had found no way of saying the little I might have had to say. And of course, having only my own silence was painful. Having one's whole blood supply changed is not a pleasant operation.

As a result, I had to survive my failure. Although I, myself, survived, the person that had lived inside me died, and was translated into a dull, conformist, disinterested, nine-to-five junior executive. The years passed and I inched my way up the salary scale until I reached security and its recognisable trappings – a little status, some small authority, my name on a door, and a pension on which to hang my hat if ever I lived to be sixty-five. But trappings so easily become traps, and security so often involves sacrifice of freedom. Like most prisoners, the day eventually arrived when I wanted to break out. Every time I gave myself a shake I felt that empty bottle of ink inside me, and the urge grew to do the transfusion operation in reverse – go back to Ireland, to my roots, and to writing – refill the bottle with some new, self-startling ink.

There seemed to be two ways of looking at my position. If I closed one eye and looked only with a cold, realistic gaze, I had a clear view of the now familiar high, black wall topped by its peg of security beckoning me to cling on to it. And if I closed the other eye and looked out of *that* one, I had a view that may not have been so strong and sharp, but at least it had some identity, some colour, some life. Which of the two views should I adopt? I pondered on both of them for some time. A long look at the security peg never moved, but the other eye-view kept changing. And its life kept changing, because it was a life of memories. Memories of Cork, the city where I had been born, and had lived for the first thirty years of my life, the city of my roots. It had, no doubt, a little change, but hardly not at all as much as I was regretting my own change. Cork would still be there, still be me, still luring my past.

So I closed both eyes, decided to return and reclaim all my memories.

Nature abhors a vacuum, and there is none in these memories. I know that the street in which I played as a child and as a youngster has always had my gratitude and never been forgotten, for Cork's Mardyke, where I was born, must have been one of the city's few picturesque, nature-blest, peaceful and character-building surroundings to grow up in.

In the first thirty years of my life there it was known by everyone as the Mardyke, though in fact it had been designed in 1720 by a city official and named as the Red House Walk after a tea-house or tea-garden in the vicinity. It was a mile long, dead straight, its span no broader than about thirty feet. At the city end traffic was barred by an iron gateway, over which was its curvilinear archway in a style of decorated tracery as if graciously apologising for its firm rejection of vehicles. Beneath its specially dressed drapes, Queen Victoria and Prince Albert rode in their royal carriage for their procession down the Mardyke on her Jubilee visit to Cork. The archway was still there in my time, but before that the barrier had sported triple gates, known as Hell, Heaven and Purgatory. However, about the time I was leaving Cork the gateway was removed and traffic allowed enter. My memory tells me that its removal took place after I departed, but perhaps I think so only because I want to. Next to the archway the corporation had provided a specially-built, pinky-red house where they installed a caretaker whose duty was to ensure that the Mardyke Walk by-laws – a copy of which was clearly displayed – were adhered to. Everyone knew the caretaker as Tim, a wizened old man with a cap and uniform, a stick and a dog. I was still a youngster when Tim died, but he even still remains in my mind.

Indeed, Tim and the gateway – I always thought of it as *his* gateway – were the only objects of note for at least another fifty yards or more. On one side there was a long row of neat-looking houses with long front gardens, neat-lawned too, but they didn't attract my notice, mainly because my childhood anticipation centred on the only shop at that end of the Mardyke. It was a very small, box-like shop with its owner, Mr Healy, always behind the counter. He sold fruit and food that I didn't want, for my target was chocolate and in summer ice-cream. I suppose Healy's could have been looked on as a tuck-shop, because directly opposite to it was a school, St Joseph's which many years earlier included as one of its pupils the young Seán Ó Faoláin.

My blend of Mardyke memories constantly jostle each other in the summer-house of my mind. Across from my home was a bumpy, uncared-for field, often muddy, beside which was the contrast of a well-prepared, well-groomed cricket pitch, and after that a park, bloom-burst in the splendiferous prime of its season. Not surprisingly, for a brief week in my every young year, the bumpy field was my daily paradise wander-and-wonder-world. Monday morning would reverberate with the deafening, clangy arrival of trucks, cars and caravans, mixing with animal ululations, roars, bellows and barks. It was Duffy's Circus making its annual visit, and as my mother knew Mr Duffy, I was allowed to mingle with them, see them erect their big tent, watch the men on their different tasks, and make sure never to miss the many animals being fed. Gazing for long periods at the horses and other denizens of the animal kingdom almost certainly started my love for and admiration of their different shapes, colours and natures. Perhaps too it was the size, the swaying trunk and policeman-like plodding steps of the elephant that established it as my favourite among dumb creatures.

Among Mr Duffy's workmen was another giant, nicknamed Tiny Tim. He was almost eight feet tall, a shapely colossus with wavy black hair and massive hands. Never once did I see any of the workmen talk to him, or him try to mix with them. I enjoyed watching him work, feeling comfortable in his company and glad that he wasn't annoyed by my presence. Children are in awe of a giant and are usually drawn to one, while grown men often see such a creature as outlandishly abnormal, sometimes menacing, and so they silently thank their own lucky stars not to be cursed with such oddity.

After I stood there for a while, Tiny Tim turned to me.

'What's your name, son?' he said.

Though I talked with him every morning that week, I remember only those first few words of that conversation. The fatherly warmth of that address – 'son' – made me feel completely at home. I told him my name, and then asked him his.

'I'm called Tiny Tim,' he answered. He didn't laugh or smile.

'Is it all right if I call you Tim?'

He laughed then.

'It'll do, son, it'll do.'

We became real friends. He always carried sweets and gave some to me. But not too many because he said too many were bad for my teeth. I wish I knew what we talked about, but whatever it was, it faded from my mind once the week ended and the circus departed. When it returned the following year, first thing in the Monday morning I ran into the field to say hello to Tim. When I couldn't find him, I asked one of the men where he was.

'Tim? That eejit? He scarpered. Went to England. Someone tried to make him into a boxer.'

'A boxer?' I wasn't sure what 'making him into a boxer' meant.

'Some boxer, Tiny Tim! He had two fights and was beaten into a pulp each time. That was the end of him.'

I didn't know what 'pulp' meant either, but I knew it sounded unpleasant.

I never saw or heard of Tim again. When I grew up and sometimes read in the sports page about two boxers slugging each other out in the ring, I thought about Tim and was glad he wasn't either of them.

Next to that rough field the cricket pitch was my special joy. In the summer, weather permitting, there'd be a match almost every evening and I would climb up on a pillar at the end of our front garden fence and sit on it as if it were a grandstand seat. Thus did cricket become my first sporting love, though on the odd occasion some lusty batsman would break our front-room window by hitting a six and my mother would warn me not to sit on the pillar in case I'd be hit by the ball. But there was no chance I'd give up my perch, because with my elevation, my eyesight was so strong that I could see right over the cricket pitch into the Sunday's Well tennis courts behind it and its adjoining billiard-table-smooth bowling-green. Sometimes a batsman's six hit would just fail to reach our garden, the ball descending from the skies and splashing into the stream across the road. As I was able to note exactly where it entered the water, I would rush over and wait for the groundsman to arrive, carrying a long pole with a net on its end, and I would proudly tell him exactly where he'd find the ball.

The stream was known as the Mardyke Stream, which it was thus christened, because being only about five feet across it could hardly be regarded as a river, but what it lacked in width, it gained in length. It flowed all the way from even before the Mardyke Walk gateway until past the cricket pitch, where it then went underground. Once when one of the boys in school asked me where I lived, I told him, just for a joke, that I lived by the sea, and for a moment he almost believed it. I could have told him that I lived by the River Lee, and even though the stream could technically be considered a tributary of the Lee, I was afraid that to give such an answer might provoke the boy's laughter. I kept quiet too about the elm-trees, a battalion of massive guardians that lined my stream for the whole of its course.

After the cricket pitch came the park, Fitzgerald's Park, a boon to me, providing a short cut to my primary school, St Mary's Shandon. It was an extensive park, and even though I never had any particular interest in flowers and plants, the splendour of the various blooms drew even me to stand and stare and marvel at them. In the grounds was the Cork Public Museum, and a number of sculptures exhibited on the lawn were welcome company for me, the park usually being empty of people at my so-early school-going hour. However, the excitement to come was the sight of the broad Lee itself which I would have to cross to reach my school. It was my good luck that no more than four years before, the ferry that had been the only means of getting to the other side had been replaced by a bridge: a long, white suspension bridge, named

the Daly Bridge, being a gift to the city from the Daly family, but
generally known as the Shaky Bridge, because by swinging from
its cables one could make the bridge sway up and down as one
crossed, as if one was riding a merry-go-round horse. The thrill of
that sensation was a constant delight. It made going to school
worthwhile.

However, it is the Mardyke Walk itself that inhabits me – the
silent stream that didn't have to be heard to tell me it was there,
its huge, trunk elms that rested their bulky bottoms against convenient walls and linked their arms together over the road in
convivial, tipsy whisperings. They were trees for climbing, trees
for knocking out pipes on, trees for getting a free view of the
cricket, trees for lullabying you to sleep at night, trees for lovers.

All that was the Mardyke Walk I knew, many, many years
ago. But it's not because I haven't seen it for so long that I talk of
it in the past tense. No – it's because I can never see again the
Mardyke of my youth. The trees are all removed, sentenced to
their death by Dutch Elm disease, and the stream has disappeared
entirely from sight, covered over in the cause of progress. Ah
well, so be it. I can still, now and again, find old Tim poking with
his stick in the hedges of my memory; the stream still flows
quietly through my thoughts; and the big, gossipy trees still ramble
and reminisce in the ghostly Mardyke of my mind.

Nowadays I often wax angry when prevented by the sounds of
today's world from recollecting certain sounds I used hear when I
was young. Today what irrupts through our open windows or
batters the closed ones from morning till night are not sounds, but
just sheer noise – stunning, piercing, thundering, deafening. The
drone of an airliner, the scream of jets, the snarl of exhaust pipes,
the blare of car radios, the screech of brakes, the wailing of
virtually useless residential burglar-alarms – all that we must live
with, live through.

In my youth there was one particular sound that delighted

me, but there is nowhere I could live now with any chance of hearing it. I can visualise where it used to come from, but today's encompassing noise makes the recall of the sound itself inaudible in my head. It came from a bandstand very near my home on a plot of open ground between the Mardyke and the Western Road, and there each week in the summer a brass band used to play.

Those were the days in Ireland when there were scores of brass bands, but even in my youth they were already beginning to disappear. Ordinary working men did ordinary working jobs by day, but when they gathered in the wooden bandstand by evening and proudly put their shining instruments to their lips, they seemed to me where I stood with so many listeners in the tree-shadowed light, the greatest, most gifted musicians in the world. And when on special occasions they marched down the Mardyke, playing their way to an election rally or a football match, they drew us all into the drilled rhythm of their step, making us experience something special about those moments of our lives. The bandstand is gone and their sound is no longer heard in the Mardyke, but it has not been forgotten by me or by many of Ireland's famous writers. It is Cork's Frank O'Connor who in his story, 'The Cornet Player Who Betrayed Ireland', described that memorable, lost world:

> Out in the sunlight ... the band formed up. Dickie Ryan, the bandmaster's son, and myself took our places at either side of the big drummer, Joe Shinkwin. Joe peered over his big drum to right and left to see if all were in place and ready; he raised his right arm and gave the drum three solid flakes; then, after the third thump the whole narrow channel of the street filled with a roaring torrent of drums and brass, the mere physical impact of which hit me in the belly. Screaming girls in shawls tore along the pavements calling out to the bandsmen, but nothing shook the soldierly solemnity of the men with their eyes almost crossed on the music before them. I've heard Toscanini conduct Beethoven, but compared with Irishtown playing 'Marching Through Georgia'

on a Sunday morning it was only like Mozart in a girls' school. The mean little houses, quivering with the shock, gave it back to us; the terraced hillsides that shut out the sky gave it back to us; the interested faces of the passers-by in their Sunday clothes from the pavements were like mirrors reflecting the glory of the music. When the band stopped and again you could hear the gapped sound of feet, and the people running and chattering, it was like a parachute jump into commonplace.

One of the most unusual memories of my teenage years in Cork was quite a common experience for me – very possibly for no one else in Cork but me. I would wake up in the middle of the night and see, framed in the narrow splink of visibility that barely squeezed through a gap in the curtains, a skull grinning at me from only two feet away. However, when that happened I didn't scream in panic and I wasn't paralysed with fear. I just turned on my other side and went off to sleep again! Nerves of steel? No, nothing like that. The fact is that I knew the skull. It's name was Yorick – naturally – and it belonged to my brother. Or to be absolutely accurate, it belonged to my brothers, for there were two of them, both older than me and both medical students. The medical course was, and still is, a very long one – even if every examination was successfully negotiated first time – and consequently, soon after my brothers joined the medical faculty, our home life quickly underwent what seemed to be a permanent change of routine, atmosphere, and environment. In the first place, there were the bones. Apart from the skull itself, there were various pieces of Yorick always lying around. The clavicle made an excellent book-rest, the patella could at a pinch be pressed into service as a temporary ash tray, the tibia and fibula were large enough to keep a book open at the correct page with a finger joint to mark the exact line, and there was a string of assorted vertebrae which could be made to dance and writhe like a skinned snake.

And then we had the medical text books themselves with

their hair-raising illustrations, the heaviest tomes I had ever seen outside of a library. Once I had got over the initial shock, it was a fascinating occupation to study the pictures of the various organs hidden away inside me and to wonder at the maze of veins and arteries, every bit as intricately assembled as the electrical system of a massive airliner.

The changes, however, didn't only concern the inanimate incidentals, for our daily routine had to undergo constant adjustments as a result of having two medical students in the family. Meals, for instance, could no longer be regarded as fixed festivals. They had to be slightly movable to fit in with the timing of lectures, the meetings of various student groups – official and unofficial – and the ever-present duty of going along to cheer the college teams in their assorted sporting activities, camogie not excepted. At night the wireless had to be kept low if my brothers were swotting in the next room, and as exam time approached, going to bed was for me a silent and lonely end to the day as I gazed on my brothers' empty beds and wondered what time they'd close their books and stagger up.

Then of course there were all the new faces floating in and out – the loud voices and cheery tones of my brothers' fellow-students, the complete and sometimes provocative shift of the subjects of conversation into hitherto undreamt-of adult fields, the constant humour and horse play – ribald, perhaps, but inoffensive – and the often liberating irreverence of the college student publications. And there were small things, small but recurring, like getting my feet tangled up in the garish college scarves which were so long that they were always slithering down off the peg in the hall, or being called in sometimes to the study-room to strip off my shirt and have my ribs tapped or a cold stethoscope plonked against my chest.

On one occasion my eldest brother said he wanted to measure my chest expansion. He put a tape measure around me and said, 'Breathe out first and keep like that for a second.' I did as directed. He took my measure, showed the tape to my other brother and they both nodded to each other. 'Now I'll measure your chest expanded,' I was told. My brother replaced the tape around me, saying, 'Now, breathe in and hold it.' I did so, the tape was removed and examined again by both of them. My eldest brother then made the announcement. 'Your normal chest measurement was thirty inches. Expanded it was twenty-seven inches.' Whereupon they both collapsed with laughter. I, needless to say, was not amused by their idea of a joke.

'*Aoibhinn beatha an scoláire*' the Gaelic poem says (the life of a student is pleasant). Well, for me the life of a student's brother was also pleasant – and exciting and rewarding too. And of course it stayed that way, because the two medical students became two doctors. So, whenever necessary, I had my own private and personal physician whom I could consult free of charge. And, what's more, if I didn't like what he said, I could just as easily get a second opinion!

When I was a lad of ten or eleven I had at different times some experience of two interesting Cork activities. One of them had a particular attraction for boys, boys of from seven to seventy. It was watching motor-racing. And the other pursuit, at which I spent two summer evenings a week for about a year, was certainly not recommended entertainment for a youngster of my age: going to the dogs.

First, as to motor-racing. This was real motor-racing, *grand prix* stuff. As far as I'm aware, nothing like it was held in Ireland before or since, but in the mid-1930s an annual International Motor Race took place in Cork at which the Stirling Mosses and Graham Hills and Jack Brabhams and Prince Bira all competed.

The race was held over the Carrigrohane Circuit just outside the city, and its six miles odd encompassed Victoria Cross, Dennehy's Cross, past Cait Sé's Lane and Hell-hole, finishing up with that marvellous high-speed stretch of nearly two miles known as the Straight Road. Needless to say, this was a major event in the calendar for all the citizens of Cork – things like film festivals and drama festivals were still unknown. The race was held on a Saturday afternoon and for two mornings before that the circuit was closed to traffic while practising took place. But if it was closed to traffic, it wasn't closed to spectators, as long as they arrived before 7 a.m. Naturally, I had taken up my vantage point on a high wall at Victoria Cross long before the scheduled time. From there I could see the cars scream down the long straight towards me before screeching, scrambling and skidding into the almost hair-bend that brought them back onto the winding part of the course. If I was lucky, some of them mightn't brake quite in time and then they'd end up scattering sand and sandbags from the padded walls that marked the corner. The smell of the petrol fumes and burning rubber, the blaze of exhausts, the visored heads behind the cockpit, the dazzling primary colours of the cars with their big, white disks and black numbers on their sides – that was champagne to a youngster.

However, if that was champagne, my other habitual escapade – going to the dogs – was rather strong beer, though in fact it was innocent enough. The greyhound track was around the corner from my home and a neighbour used take me with him, passing me through the turnstile free because of my extreme youth. I was no trouble at all to him; I placed myself at the top of the stand, thoroughly fascinated with the strange world I found there. All these big men with their big voices, big smiles, big gestures, big money, and big groans enthralled me. And the bookies with their big satchels and not-so-big odds, in no time their patter and performances were as entertaining as a stage show.

After a while I was more than just a spectator. Not a gambler of course – two to one in pennies wouldn't have been much help to any bookmaker's finances – but I became an avid student of form. I studied the evening paper with the trials and times of the competing greyhounds, I went to watch them parade before each race and evolved my own method of judging their fitness or

otherwise, and I made my selection. And I was astonishingly
successful. A few times I even went through the card – all seven
winners!

Of course it all came to an end when the man at the turnstile
eventually said that I was growing too big to be let in free. For a
while after that I still studied the programme in the evening paper,
but my magic touch of so often choosing the right favourite seemed to have deserted me – nothing but ridiculous outsiders kept
coming up. So I never went to the dogs again. One day a long
time afterwards I happened to turn over the newspaper's sports
page and my eye was caught by the headline of the greyhound
racing results: 'All seven favourites oblige at Cork'.

When I was a lad I was a great one for going to the cinema.
At first I didn't mind what picture was showing. What always
thrilled me was the magic spell that descended when I left the
bright, sunlit streets and noisy traffic, and entered the mysterious,
exciting, hushed atmosphere of semi-darkness and long, carpeted
aisles. I liked the feeling of being alone, yet in a crowd; and the
jacky-dandy finger of light from the usher's torch (there were no
usherettes then) was like a leprechaun beckoning me on towards
the crock of gold.

I remember my first two visits – or, to be exact, I remember
the first time I didn't go and the first time I did. The first time I
didn't go nearly broke my heart. My eldest brother – five years my
senior and a hardened film-fan – was taking my other brother –
eighteen months older than myself – on the latter's very first visit
to the cinema. (There was yet another brother but he was still
unborn, and when he did arrive on the scene he took this whole
business to the fair altogether, ending up not merely as a filmgoer
but as a film maker!) Anyway, the picture my brothers were going
to see – I remember the name to this day – was *Trader Horn* and
it was showing in the Coliseum, known to all Corkonians as 'the
Col'. Well, I wept buckets, but it was no use. My parents wouldn't
let me join the party, saying the film had lions and tigers and

elephants that would frighten me. My goodness, haven't parents any savvy at all? Lions and tigers and elephants! Sure they're the staff of life to an eight-year-old! I think the truth was that they had to maintain the status of my older brother. It wouldn't do for us both to go to the pictures for the first time together – I had to wait my turn. I suppose nowadays, in some circles anyway, that's known as maintaining the differential.

I recall my first real visit far less clearly. I believe the Pavilion was the cinema and all I remember of the film was an engine rushing out of the screen and frightening me out of my seat and right out into the street. But it didn't take me long to get my bearings and in no time at all I was frequently in the afternoon queue for 'The Fourpennies'.

The three Cork cinemas I remember are no longer there, gone this many a year but far from forgotten. They were the Imperial, the Washington, and the Assembly Rooms. The Imperial was, I think, burnt down; the Washington definitely was burnt down and another cinema, the Ritz, was built on its site, though it didn't last very long; and the Assembly Rooms – or the Assaah, as it was called – went out of business.

The point about these three cinemas was that they were very much in the third division, so to speak, a bit primitive, not to say rough. They had wooden benches in the cheaper parts where I used sit. The projector frequently broke down – it was a bit of a disappointment if it didn't. And the romantic passages of the film were the signal for bedlam to break loose and the excuse for some heavy, innocent horseplay with the person next to you – who, if you had displayed any cuteness at all in choosing your seat, would be female and about your own age. It was all part of the serious business of growing up, which is why I can look back on it nostalgically. Nowadays of course, TV and the films being produced have completely changed both the cinemas and the youngsters. But for me, recollection of these old Cork cinemas and of the cry 'Fourpennies Full' brings back a world in which past, present and future were a screen of glamour and the only problem was what on earth could one do with oneself on a Sunday afternoon.

'Beauty rests in the eye of the beholder' is, of course, only too true, but what is often not realised is that there is far more beauty to be found than immediately meets the eye of the beholder. I have little difficulty in deciding whether, say, a painting or a particular sunset has any beauty for me – or, to take the subject out of the realm of the specifically visual – whether I find a certain song or poem beautiful. But very often I may look at something quite utilitarian or functional or merely accidental, and because it is not part of its purpose to be beautiful I may completely miss the beauty hidden in it.

For example, I have at one time or another been struck by the pictures that seem suddenly to be formed by a chance arrangement of the clouds in the sky, or I've stared into a roaring fire or its dying embers and seen the outline of a face. This kind of common occurrence is, however, fleeting, for the clouds and the fire alter their composition so rapidly. But if I were an artist I'd by now have a couple of sketchbooks full of the faces I've seen, not in the too quickly disappearing clouds or flames, but simply in carpets and curtains. I'm continually being surprised by the puckish little fairies I find lurking in the patterns of carpets and by the sleek-haired, silken maidens whose faces hide in the folds and shadows of a curtain. Sometimes the search for hidden beauty of this sort gives me days when I become an inveterate carpet-gazer or curtain-starer.

But in fact the most common form of hidden beauty, and sometimes the most rewarding, is what is known as the 'found poem'. It can be found in a newspaper, a legal document, a telephone directory, anywhere where the original intention of writing was not poetic. It retains the same words as the original though they might be rearranged into lines to draw attention to their poetry.

The most famous example of the 'found poem' is that piece of art criticism by Walter Pater about the Mona Lisa which so struck W. B. Yeats that he merely arranged it as poetry instead of prose and published it in the *Oxford Book of English Verse*. Of course, Pater was an acknowledged master of style, so it isn't very surprising if a piece of his prose turns out to be poetry. But how about this exquisite little unintended poem from a travel guide:

> Seasons in Uruguay
> are the opposite of ours.
> Their summer is our winter
>
> and vice versa …
> It's exceedingly windy
> in the Spring,
> and children go to the beaches
> to fly kites.
> The climate is bright, dry
> and invigorating.
> Snow is unknown.

And read this 'found poem' about ships:

> Cockleshell, foldboat, cockboat, lifeboat,
> Long-boat, jolly-boat, fly-boat, bumboat,
> Picket boat, pinnace, cutter, gig,
> Wherry, ferry, ferry-boat, canal boat,
> Hooker, bilander, towboat, tug,
> Gabbard, nobby, Bawley, cog,
> Dory, fishing smack, herring fisher, trow,
> Saic, caique, gallivat, dhow.
>
> (Very fast)

Motorboat, speedboat, picket boat, rowboat,
Steamboat, paddle-boat, river-boat, showboat,
Pleasure boat, house boat, ferry-boat, towboat.

(Softly, slowly)

Gondola, coracle, currach, canoe,
Kayak, umiak, proa, prahu ...
Catamaran!

If I'd been told that that was by John Masefield I'd have swallowed it – hook, line and sinker. In fact it was dug out of *Roget's
Thesaurus of English Words and Phrases*.

Last Request

As I was now nearing the conclusion of this book, I was also nearing the end of Aaron and Catherine's association. When the book is finished, their story will have to end too. But as I wrote when I brought them together, I referred to the way a character whom the writer has created often takes over, directs his or her own course. Thinking about that began to disturb me. Disturb? Yes, because by inventing a fictional character I suddenly found myself trussed up in religio-philosophical knots. By being born as an Orthodox Jew, I was supposed to believe I had been given life by God, and in due course I ran into the brick wall of free will. Well, I long ago made up my own mind about that problem, but the coming together – no, the putting together by me – of Aaron and Catherine gave me not merely pause, but occasionally worrying self-doubts. By creating fictional characters, was I behaving as some sort of man-God? I suppose I was, because when a writer introduces any such characters, he becomes a man-God of fiction, though that's neither a here nor there role. However, sometimes when a book ends, particular characters do live on. How and where? Mostly in many readers' memories of what happened to them in the book. Also, in some cases there are readers who project them, wonder what could have been their future, their after-life of the finished book. Indeed in recent years some established writers have come upon in university or library archives a bygone manuscript of an unfinished novel, and have completed it for the long dead original writer.

So when I have written the last page of the last chapter about Aaron, will that be the end of him – and of me in my man-God role? That was certainly my intention, and certainly still is too. Yet there's Catherine, what about her? She started as a journalist-amanuensis, which is what I meant for her. But once she joined up with Aaron, she turned out to be far more than just a scrivener. If that's all she had been, she'd have stayed behind her desk at the *Irish Examiner*. Indeed, I was extremely happy when she got on so well with Aaron from the very first moment, and he with her. What's more, she never once tried to upstage him. She kept the story of her own life completely from him, and from me too, apart from a very few brief details in response to an early half-enquiry from Aaron. In addition, I was careful to ask nothing more of her than to play her part, for I knew that that part had to be a minor speaking one rather than being just a fly on the wall. And how well she played it, so sympathetically and with such honest interest, that I couldn't force myself to play the heavy and prevent her from being herself – a warm, understanding, artless girl.

When her phone rang on the morning which presumably would be the last day of her assignment about the story of Cork's Jews, it was Aaron at the other end.

'Aaron! What is it, Aaron? Are you not well?' she asked urgently.

'Not at all, my dear. I'm in perfect form. But I have a business call to make this morning and I also want to drop into the library to consult something, so I'll be tied up until about noon. You and I, we don't have any more special places I need to show you, but I have some odd bits of history to pass on to you that you might want to use. So why don't we meet for lunch, if it suits you, and afterwards we could go back to my home and spend a comfortable afternoon there talking and tying up any loose ends. How about that?'

'Perfect, except that I'd much prefer if we had lunch in your place rather than sit in a noisy, busy restaurant. I like making lunch for you, and for myself too. I'll bring the food. Now no argument, I insist. You'll be home by one, won't you?'

'There you go again. You open your mouth and beat me down. How can I refuse? Honestly, I'd prefer it anyway. I'll be home before one. Thank you, my dear girl.'

'A pleasure, dear man, a pleasure,' with her cheeky laugh. 'See you soon.'

Going home after completing his business, Aaron was just about to buy two bottles of wine, red and white, because he didn't know which colour Catherine preferred, and then he remembered that she'd have her car, so wouldn't drink anyway. So chocolates, that would fit the bill instead. He hid them in his bedroom, and as soon as they had finished their meal and relaxed in the living room, out came the beribboned box.

'I'm hoping, my dear,' he said, 'that like me you are at least a little prone to a sweet tooth.'

'I must admit I am, but I'm careful not to over-indulge. One or two will suit me, thank you. A really pleasant final course before you tell me what further information you have for me. I have my jotter with me to make the odd note.'

'Good girl, good girl, and what I want to start with is something that I told you when we visited the Marina, but I thought I should check on it. That's why I went to the library this morning. It's about Henry Ford.'

'Oh, Cork's great inventor,' Catherine said as she wrote his name in her jotter.

'Yes, well, an Irish source – which I happen to have – said that Henry Ford "came from a village known as Ballinascarty, thirty miles west of Cork", and that's what I told you. It didn't mention the date of his birth. What's more, Catherine, what's more, the big Biographical Dictionary I have says he was born in the US.

'Well, lying in bed during the night I couldn't sleep because that contradiction worried me – which is why I went to the library this morning. Fortunately, they had not only one, but two biographies of Henry Ford, and the very first thing each of them told me was quite a surprise. The first one was published in April 1946, and the opening sentence of its Foreword is "On July 30, 1946, an eminent American will round his eighty-third milestone". And the second one, published in 1969, gave the exact same date – but you don't, my dear, have to calculate his birth date because they both give it as 30 July 1863. And it didn't take place in Ballinascarty. Far from it. In 1847 three Ford brothers who work- ed their farm in Co. Cork emigrated together to America as re- fugees from Ireland's Great Famine. They settled on a farm in Dearborn, near Detroit. One of them, William, married in 1862, and Henry came into the world a year later. So Cork's Henry Ford was a first generation American, but clearly he didn't forget his heritage when he founded Ford's in Cork. What sayest thou, Catherine?'

'Well, well, well,' Catherine muttered as she finished writing. '"Well, well, well" is only half of it. Ready for the next bit?'

'Proceed, master,' she laughed.

'Well,' Aaron started, then laughed and added, 'there's one more "well", but at least it's a good one. I told you that Ford was a known anti-Semite, that I had read about it somewhere years ago but couldn't remember where. Well – my goodness, there's that word again, but at least there's good clear water in it – both of this morning's biographies deal with that matter. It seems that Henry Ford set up a weekly newspaper, or possibly a magazine, called the *Dearborn Independent* and for two years it carried anti- Semitic articles. They were not written by Ford himself, but by a Hearst newspaper man, and eventually Ford faced a libel suit for one million dollars damages for publishing the articles about the activities of a Jewish attorney. Before the trial, Henry Ford be- came convinced that the articles could not be substantiated and he made a public apology.

'In his apology – and I made for you, Catherine, a copy of the important part of his apology – "Mr Henry Ford did not participate personally in the publication of the articles and has no personal knowledge of what was said in them. He, of course, deprecated greatly that any facts that were published in a periodical so closely associated with his name in the minds of the public should be untrue." It's completely up to you, Catherine, whether you want to include this in your story, but certainly it made me happy. Our Henry is back in my top list. The only mistake he made was not being born in Cork, but I suppose I can't blame him for that, can I?'

'You certainly can't, Aaron, and I'll certainly use that story about him, just in case there's anyone in Cork who knows only the wrong version.'

'Good. Now having got that off my mind, there are the other bits and pieces for you that are of some interest, but not exactly sweet and happy, so have another chocolate first.'

'I will if you will, Aaron, but that's my quota, OK?'

'OK Catherine. Whatever you say.'

They both studied the chocolate box to search out their favourites, munched away diligently, and then Catherine sat back for Aaron's further tales.

'The early twenties in Ireland and particularly in Cork, we had the British soldiers and the infamous Black and Tans. I was only about five at the time, too young to remember seeing any of the trouble – I imagine I was never taken into the city then, probably too risky and dangerous. But when I was a bit older and the soldiers had all departed, I used hear stories from the Jewish men who lived in Jewtown. One thing they all agreed was that they were never rounded up or threatened by the British army, because once they knew you were a Jew, they took it for granted that you were in no way involved with Irish politics and so weren't the enemy. Little did they know that the Jews in Ireland were all agin' them. The Irish had made them feel at home when so many of them were refugees escaping from persecution, and anyway, the cruelty and savagery of the Black and Tans was hated by everyone.

'The Tans, in fact, were responsible for the death of one member of the Cork Jewish community, and in a way many people would have called it a sort of accident, sort of not deliberate. One night they broke into a shop in Tuckey Street that was owned by a Jew. But whether they knew that, was anyone's guess. The owner and his wife lived over the shop, and they were asleep when the noise of the break-in woke them up. When the Tans burst into their bedroom, the owner's wife screamed, and shouted "Don't shoot, we're Jewish". But she was so terrified that she had a heart attack and died immediately. It was reported in the *Cork Examiner* some time in the very early 1920s, and if they still have copies of these years' papers, you may want to look it up – though it would take a lot of time and trouble, I suppose.'

'I could ask our librarian,' Catherine essayed. 'He might know if our archives go that far back.'

'While you're at it, you might ask him about the *Lusitania*. They're bound to have a report on it. As you'll know, the *Lusitania* was one of Britain's greatest liners. It was torpedoed and sunk by a German U-boat off the Old Head of Kinsale on 7 May 1915. Civilian loss of life was 1,198 passengers and crew, 140 being American citizens.'

'Has it got something to do with Cork?'

'It has. Many of its passengers were killed or drowned. Five of them were Jewish, and they're buried in the Cork Jewish cemetery.'

'Who were they? Wouldn't it be possible to find their names if we went there?'

'I don't know, but I doubt it.'

'Why?'

'For two reasons. Firstly, the place is locked up. There is someone who I believe has the job of taking care of it fairly regularly, but I've no idea who he is. Perhaps some department of the Cork City or County Council would know. However, I very much doubt that they'd allow a stranger to go there, a complete stranger with no relations buried there.'

'But we could go together, couldn't we?'

'No, Catherine, we couldn't,' Aaron replied.

'Why not?' Catherine asked in surprise.

'For the second reason, my dear. It's because of my name.'

'Your name? But it's Aaron Cohen! You're a Jew! No one could possibly say you aren't.'

'That's right, Catherine, but the name "Cohen" comes from the Hebrew word *kohen*, meaning a priest. In the Israelites' Bible times, Aaron, the brother of Moses, was the first priest, and in much later times any Jew with the name "Cohen" could regard himself as a *kohen*, a priest. However, one of the Jewish laws is that a *kohen* is not allowed to enter a graveyard unless the corpse is a near relative. He must stay apart from the burial ground.'

'So you're really a priest?'

'Well,' Aaron explained, 'I never regarded myself as a priest just because of my name.'

'So why wouldn't you go to the graveyard?'

'Ah, that brings me to the bit of business I had to do this morning. I went to see my solicitor, the man I always keep in touch with and he keeps in touch with me. I phone him every morning so as to tell him I'm still in the land of living. We have an arrangement about it because he takes care of all my affairs.'

Aaron fell silent for some moments. Catherine waited for him to continue.

'I've been thinking. Although I feel very well, being my age there's no knowing the day or the hour when I'll wake up and find myself dead.'

'Oh, Aaron, Aaron,' Catherine laughed, 'that's just like a Jewish joke, waking up to find yourself dead!'

'Anyway, when I die, I couldn't be buried in Cork because

there'd be no one to bury me or to mourn for me.'

'No one, Aaron? What about me? I'd miss you,' Catherine said quietly, almost in a whisper.

'Thank you, Catherine,' Aaron said. He took out his handkerchief, blew his nose, and added, 'Thank you, dear girl.'

'But Aaron, I don't want to depress you with such talk, but if you couldn't be buried in Cork, where can you be buried? In Dublin?'

'No, not Dublin either.'

Catherine looked at him, her brow wrinkled with astonishment.

'I've always felt that I'd rather be cremated than buried, but I hadn't done anything about it until today when I saw my solicitor. The surprise is that there's no crematorium in Cork, so he'll make the arrangements in Dublin, pay whatever it costs, and my account will refund him. That'll leave my mind at rest. I'd rather be burned upstairs than downstairs.'

Catherine wondered just for a moment and then cottoned on.

'Oh, you mean on the ground instead of below ground.'

'That's exactly it. Who'd fancy hell? Not that I believe it exists.'

'I don't either,' Catherine emphatically declared. 'But when you come to think of it,' she mock-seriously added, 'look at all the volcanoes in the world that suddenly erupt in flames every now and again. Maybe they're really coming from hell after all.'

'Oh, aren't you clever, smart alec. Maybe they're coming from the constantly increasing numbers of our world's sinners who have to do overtime stoking the furnaces to make enough room for hell's growing population. Anyway, one way or another life is just a short journey from creation to cremation. There endeth the lesson.'

'Just one other thing, Aaron. When – when you have to go to Dublin, you won't be going alone. I'll go with you, so give your solicitor my phone number and tell him to keep in touch with me.'

Aaron rose, went to Catherine, took her hands in his and kissed each of them.

'Thank you, my very dear girl. Thank you.'

'Now how about a cuppa? Would you like one?'

'I certainly would. I feel a bit dry after all my talking, and I happen to have a little bit more to tell you too.'

True to form, Catherine had the tea ready within minutes and produced an assortment of plain and mixed biscuits. They drank and nibbled slowly, chatted about this and that, and then Catherine put the delph and biscuits aside, took up her jotter, and said, 'Now, Aaron, what else is it you have to tell me?'

'For one thing, you can put your jotter away. What I want to tell you doesn't need to be written down. Just relax, and listen.'

Aaron began to scratch his chin, as if unsure how to start. Then he found his voice.

'The main reason I went to see my solicitor this morning was to talk to him about my will. I made it only quite recently, but when I gave up my tailoring business many years ago, I had plenty of money and no one to give it to – the last of my Jewish friends were all dead. So I left it to charity, shared it between hospitals. And this morning I told my solicitor that I had decided to change the will. I gave him new instructions, he wrote them down, and he'll have the new will ready in a few days.'

Aaron paused, then went on. 'When I die, Catherine, this home of mine will be yours –'

'Aaron!'

'Ssh, Catherine. This place will be yours, to live in or, if you wish, to sell it. Whatever you like. I didn't cancel the bequests to the hospitals but I just reduced them. They'll get a fair amount of money anyway, because – well, the truth is, Catherine, that I'm very wealthy indeed. It's all been amassed over a long life and a successful business. And as I told you about my dear wife, she had been left a lot of money by one of her grandfathers. Before we married she made her will, and then, when she died so tragically, her fortune came to me.

'Would there be any more tea in the pot, Catherine? If there isn't, don't bother. It's just that speechifying about my will is embarrassing.'

Catherine, in a daze, checked the teapot. 'Yes, there is. But let me heat it up a bit.'

'No, no. Just fill my cup. I want to finish what I'm saying.'

She poured him a cupful. Aaron drank almost all of it and put it down. He wiped his lips. Then his eyes. And then he went over to the sideboard, took up his wedding photograph, and with his back still turned, he said, 'Catherine, when I die, my money won't any longer be mine. It will be yours.'

He heard a cry, like a small, choked scream. Before he could move, Catherine had her arms around him, her face against his tear-wet cheeks.

'No, Aaron, no. You can't do that. You can't.'

He took her back to her chair and sat down himself. 'I wanted to do it, dear Catherine, so I did it. What it is, Catherine, is that you are so very special – more even than that. The truth is … the truth is, if I had been lucky enough to have a daughter, I would have wanted her to be exactly the same as you.'

'Aaron, Aaron, what can I do? What can I say?'

'Nothing. Say nothing. Let us sit back for a while and just rest. The emotion is a bit too much for me. Maybe it's because of my age. Or perhaps I'm just not used to it.'

Aaron stayed silent for at least a minute. He kept looking straight at Catherine, as if he was somehow seeing her for the first time. She wondered why he was staring right into her eyes. What was he trying to find?

'No,' he suddenly said. 'I can't keep quiet. I can't keep the rest of it for another time. Would you do something for me? Go into the corridor past the kitchen. On its right is the door to my bedroom, and directly across from it there's another door. I'd like you to go into that room, have a good look around it, and then tell me what you think of it. Would you do that, Catherine?'

'Certainly. Of course I would.'

She left him, and Aaron waited for her return. It took her almost five minutes before she came back.

'Aaron, what a beautiful room! A baby's room! Everything is just exquisite. The wallpaper is a delight, all little animals in colour, flowers and trees like painted scenes. And bright, lively curtains. A fireplace, and above it an old mantlepiece with photographs of you and your wife. And that cot, so delicately designed, so different, and little baby toys. I've never seen anything like it, Aaron.'

Catherine was about to say the room was like a dream, but she managed to stop herself just in time. For Aaron it must have been a tragic nightmare, she thought.

'Do you have a woman come in to keep it neat and clean?'

'No, I do it myself,' Aaron told her. 'No one else has ever been in it. When my wife became pregnant and when she decided to go over to London and tell her parents about it so that they might become reconciled, she told me that she was certain our child would be a girl. She had no doubt. She said she knew we'd have a daughter. And so, before she left Cork, she had the baby's room prepared exactly as you have just seen it. You seem to have liked it, don't you?'

'Oh, Aaron, how could anyone not like it.'

'Sit down, Catherine. I have just one thing else to tell you.'

She went back to her armchair.

'Catherine, you're an orphan and I'm an orphan. Forget my age. I live in a very comfortable home. You live in a single room. Would you consider coming to live here? You're going to own this place no matter if you have to wait for me to be a hundred. You could live here just as soon as that room is re-done, in whatever way you want it. Believe me, I'm not just saying this so as to persuade you, but honestly, every time I pass that door, I want to go into the room, and surely by now I should forget what's in there.'

Catherine was stunned by what she was hearing. Her head rose, as if she was looking up to heaven, mind-blown, astonished. She closed her eyes, held her face in her two hands.

Aaron's voice didn't stop.

'If you were to live here, your life would still be your own. If you have friends, you naturally could entertain them here – as long as this old man wouldn't put them off. If you have anything you want to ask me about, anything at all, just ask. But not immediately. First, give yourself a chance to think of what I've said, and when you have decided, we could meet, or if you'd prefer to phone me, or even write me a letter – just give me your answer. If it's no, don't worry. We'll always be friends. And you have my sworn word that nothing would make me think of changing my will back just because you'd prefer not to live here. You are special to me, Catherine, very special, as long as I live. Now, I've said everything I want to say.'

Catherine's hands were shaking.

'Oh Aaron, Aaron, what can I say?'

'I told you – think about it. As long as you like. Tomorrow, the day after, I'll wait for your answer.'

Catherine stopped the tremor of her hands. She was suddenly herself again.

'Aaron, you have already waited, waited through a long and lonely life. I've also waited through a lonely life, though nowhere as long as yours. We're both orphans – you a friendless one, apart from me; I – well, I've only one or two acquaintances in the *Examiner*, but you're the only real friend I found since the day we met.'

'You don't mean …? What are you saying, Catherine?'

'Aaron, I couldn't be so cruel as to make you wait for another second. My heart and my mind say yes.'

She went to him and hugged him. They both cried, then laughed.

'I suppose I'm much too young to be your daughter, Aaron,' Catherine said light-heartedly, 'but better still, I'll be your grand-daughter.'

Aaron hugged her again and kissed her closed eyes.

'There's an old proverb, Catherine, that isn't always true. But sometimes it is. It's "Everything comes to he who waits".'

Epilogue

T. H. Huxley, a nineteenth-century scientist and writer, grand-father of novelist Aldous Huxley, said 'Autobiographies are essentially works of fiction, whatever biographies may be.' As I explained – both to myself as well as to readers – in my double-sided prologue to this book, what I intended to write was a second volume of autobiography mixed in with a historiette of the almost defunct Cork Jewish community. Of course what I needed for the teller was a character old enough to be able to retail sufficient and sufficiently interesting extracts from the more than century old Cork Jews' story.

Where did Aaron come from, or how? I didn't clone him – if I had, we would have been genetically identical. That, we certainly weren't; he didn't come from me, he just came to me, and he quickly became both a sort of Jewish seanachie-historian, and an old man with a missing life. He found a missing life, a late one, but a deserved one.

This book is ended now, but has it ended for Aaron, or Catherine? I don't know. I only know that I came to love them both.